Move Into
Your Magnificence

101 Invitations
to a Life of Passion and Joy

DR. BARY FLEET

First Stillwater River Publications Edition 2020.

Library of Congress Control Number 2019917519

ISBN-13: 978-1-950339-54-9

1 2 3 4 5 6 7 8 9 10

Written by Dr. Bary Fleet.
Cover photo by Melissa Lyons. www.Melissa-Lyons.com

Published by Stillwater River Publications, Pawtucket, RI, USA.

Publisher's Cataloging-In-Publication Data
(Prepared by The Donohue Group, Inc.)

Names: Fleet, Bary, author.
Title: Move into your magnificence : 101 invitations to a life of passion and joy / Dr.
    Bary Fleet.
Description: First Stillwater River Publications edition. | Pawtucket, RI, USA :
    Stillwater River Publications, 2020.
Identifiers: ISBN 9781950339549
Subjects: LCSH: Self-actualization (Psychology)--Anecdotes. | Joy--Anecdotes. | Life-
    -Anecdotes. | LCGFT: Anecdotes.
Classification: LCC BF637.S4 F54 2020 | DDC 158.1--dc23

*The views and opinions expressed in this book are solely those of the author
and do not necessarily reflect the views and opinions of the publisher.*

Dedication

This is dedicated to Christy and Tyler—
whose magnificence never ceases to amaze me!

Table of Contents

SELF-ACTUALIZATION

MEDITATIONS AND MEDIATIONS

Acknowledgments

I owe so much to so many: first and foremost, to my wife Debbie for her unwavering support, inspiration, patience and feedback throughout this process; Kathy Robbins from Tri-Mom Productions, who looked at me and saw a triathlete instead of just an old guy who was out-of-shape, over-weight; Heather Sischo and the Psycho Sischo Crazies from Fitness Adventure, who saw in me the potential to celebrate my seventieth birthday at Fenway Park, completing a Spartan Trifecta; Bryant University for making available their semi-annual Writers' Retreats; Steve Harrison and his amazing team from Quantum Leap who guided me through every step of this process; Dr. Christopher Westgate, Laura Kohl, Stephanie Carter, Jackie Greenstein Casey, and Alice Gregory Supinsky for being my Beta readers; Melissa Lyons for her patience and creativity with the cover photo; and the countless people I am privileged to call "friend" for their encouragement along the way.

Introduction

Many of my favorite childhood memories are of a little Methodist church in a small community in Western Pennsylvania. We lived on one side and the parsonage was on the other side. Even now, I can smell the musty basement where we had Sunday School. I remember the wires strung between the metal posts supporting the beams for the floor above suspending the curtains used to divide the area into classrooms.

The church shaped and formed me in ways for which I will be forever grateful. But I was a thinker and as I got older so much of the church's teaching didn't make sense to me. The Virgin Birth was one: How could the Holy Spirit impregnate a woman, causing her to give birth to a human? Salvation was another: If God so loved the world, how is it that salvation was available only through a peasant carpenter born a couple of thousand years ago in a small town in Israel? Would this all-loving God leave everyone else on the planet in the dark about how to "get saved?" What about the spiritual practices of the Native Americans, the Buddhists, and the Hindi's, just to name a few? I didn't understand some of the teachings, and no one could give me a satisfying answer.

"The Christian Agnostic," by Leslie Weatherhead was a book that helped me tremendously in my adolescence. He observed that there are some concepts we can know and others that we don't understand yet. He proposed that anytime we came across a question we can't answer, we simply file that away until an intellectually satisfying answer was revealed.

I went through the course of study and was granted my "License to Preach" by the Methodist Church while in my late teens, and I spent two decades as an ordained minister of the United Methodist Church. Even so, I continued to feel haunted by some of the theological teachings.

The concept of truth with a small "t" and Truth with a capital "T" helped me also. Truth with a capital T referred to a concept that was true for everyone, everywhere, and for all time. For example: "God is Love," and since we are all created by some life force (God), God must love everyone – no exceptions! I learned that through the Methodist church, but I reckoned that to be universally True.

I also struggled with the notion of how prayer works. When I was in the sixth grade, we moved from Pennsylvania to Georgia. I grew up in the Bible Belt. I watched sports teams huddle in prayer before a game, praying that God would let them win. It didn't make sense to me that God was more invested in one team winning than the other. Would God measure the faith and number of prayers for each them, and decide the winner and loser based on that? How is it that some prayers get answered and others don't? Why are some people miraculously cured and others succumb to their illnesses? The often-given answer was that sometimes God simply says "No" to a prayer. "But WHY?" I wanted to scream. "Some things we just don't understand" was another answer – and that one I could accept.

I knew other cultures prayed, but I knew they weren't praying to the God that I learned about because they didn't even know "Him." That was another question: How is it that God is male? Other cultures worshipped feminine gods. Had they just missed the memo that God is a man?

I also discovered that each faith tradition seemed to have its own "master teacher." So, I started looking for commonalities among various religions, thinking that if a practice or belief showed up in a majority, if not all of them, this was evidence to me of some universal truth, Truth with a capital T.

In some ways I am embarrassed by some of the judgmental beliefs I adopted along the way, but I am also proud, as I look back, to see how far I have come in terms of how my view the world and of "God" has expanded.

There is more to the story, but I left the United Methodists in part because of their teaching and doctrine around homosexuality. I then spent almost two decades as a pastor in the United Church of Christ because of their "Open and Affirming" doctrine. I left the United Church of Christ in part because, while my beliefs are still rooted in the teaching Christ and of the Bible, I came to understand those teachings from a metaphorical standpoint rather than a literal and traditional interpretation. Certainly, there were other forces at work, but underneath was this on-going quest for Truth.

This is ultimately what led me to the Centers for Spiritual Living and Quantum Physics, through which I have become a licensed Religious Science Practitioner. This is in the "New Thought" tradition (not to be confused with New Age), which finds Truth at the intersection of religion, science and philosophy.

I call myself as a "Religious Scientist." We live in a lawful universe and I want to understand more deeply how these laws work.

There is a universal Truth about how everything in the universe works, aspects of which we continue to discover. Think about it: The people in Old Testament times could have had electric lights, if they had a better understanding of the laws of electricity. Jesus' followers could have flown from Jerusalem to Rome instead of sailed there, if they had a better understanding of the laws of aerodynamics. These laws of physics haven't changed since the moment of creation. Down through the centuries we have simply come to understand more and more about how the laws of the natural world work.

It is also my conclusion that this One Power of the universe is creative and fundamentally loving. So, we aren't punished for anything by some judgmental "Guy in the Sky," but rather every behavior does have lawful consequences, but they are *consequences,* not punishment from God. When we are in harmony with the way the Universe works, our lives are full of light and love, of joy and peace, and of beauty and goodness.

As a part of the created universe, we – I contend – have what some have called a sacred core which longs to express itself. Some might call this the Christ-center, or the God-within. I am calling it our Inner Magnificence. We have it from the moment of conception. What baby isn't beautiful and magnificent, each in its own way!

As we go through life, we get the message that we aren't so

magnificent. A university study found that the average two-year old hears the word "No!" four hundred times a day! What is the average two-year old doing? Being an average two-year old, exploring the world.

As we continue to be judged and criticized for just being ourselves, for being curious about the world we live in, on some level we get the message that there is something wrong with us. That is when we find ways to protect our confused and hurt feelings. As we grow and develop, what we show the world is our accumulated layers of protection. Some have psychologists have called this the "false self," because underneath the "true self" is still there. It is always there! No matter how traumatic the experiences are that we endure, this Inner Magnificence never gets damaged. It remains latent, waiting to be tapped into, waiting to lead us into lives of joy and peace. It is full of creativity and great potential.

I think of the analogy of a geode. On the outside, we all look ordinary, like a rock, but when the geode is broken open, when our sense of shame is cracked, like the crystals in a geode, our inner beauty is revealed.

Too many people – I know, because I was one of them – go through life with poor self-esteem. We spend untold amounts of energy trying to cover up our real selves for fear of being judged and humiliated. We go through life covered with self-imposed layers of protection.

Each of us falls into one of three categories: some of us have connected with our Inner Magnificence and the world recognizes us for it; some of us would like to think there is something more inside us, but we're afraid to let down our defenses long enough to tap into it; and some of us have been so beaten down by life, that we live lives of quiet desperation, just doing our best to get from one day to the next.

So, if you find yourself in this first category, please go out into the world, committed to helping others to connect with their own Inner Magnificence. If you are in either of the latter categories, please read, and accept, the following invitations.

The extent to which you do is the extent to which you'll be able to say, "I feel good about being me!" … and that's a promise!

P.S. I am so grateful for purchasing this book that I want to offer some gifts to you.

Go to www.DrBaryFleet.com/BookBonuses.

Enter your email address and I will send you ABSOLUTELY FREE:

1) A downloadable audible copy of this book.

2) A set of five of more recent articles including:
   a. *Who are You Becoming*
   b. *A Trail of Litter: What does yours look like?*
   c. *The Price of Convenience*
   d. *A Million Little Things*
   e. *The Shame I Carry*

3) Check my Coaching Page for a free thirty-minute coaching session.

If I can ever be of service to you, please don't hesitate to reach out! There's nothing I'd like to do more than to help you or your organization connect with YOUR INNER MAGNIFICENCE!

My Story

I was a big baby, but grew up being small for my age. When I started elementary school, I was the smallest boy in my class, and stayed that way until the seventh grade.

Even though my birthday is in November, I started first grade when I was five. My family had me tested, and I was deemed academically ready. I couldn't wait! I loved school! I was the kind of kid who was offended when the teacher didn't assign homework, because I knew the only way to learn was by doing homework. So, when the teacher didn't assign any, I would go home, sit on the floor in front of my little chalkboard, and make up homework.

I have only good memories of my life until October of second grade. Just as my family was sitting down for supper, I heard the town fire alarm go off. We lived in a small town with an all-volunteer fire department. What little boy doesn't like sirens? I jumped up from the table, ran outside, and looked down the street to see where the fire truck was going. Then, I saw it—crossing our street—and I knew; the ONLY place it could be headed was the school!

I ran inside, yelled to my parents that the school was on fire. I ran back outside, across the street, and climbed the fence into Hoover's pasture. Then I went as close to the school as I could. In the meantime, my dad joined the other men of the town fighting the fire. I was close enough to see everything that was happening. I was close enough that I could feel the heat from the fire on my face.

I stood there, six years old, and realized that the fire was too big and the resources to fight the fire were too small, and the fire was going to win. It was a two-story, all wood structure; it was the same school my mother had attended when she was in elementary school.

I didn't realize it until some of the "big kids" called attention to me but, as I was taking in the reality of what was happening, I had silent tears streaming down my cheeks. The big kids—that means the third and fourth graders—asked me why I was crying, and with great sincerity replied, "We aren't going to have school tomorrow!" They all laughed at me and went away chanting, "No more school! No more school! No more school!"

Decades later, through lots of therapy, I realized that was the day I made a resolution: "Don't let anybody know what you are really feeling, because they will laugh at you!"

Fast forward to fifth grade. We had moved, and I was now living in a different school district, one much larger. There was an elementary school, a middle school, and the high school that my dad had attended, all in the same complex.

One day, there was a school assembly and I was elated as I walked in with my class and saw all the instruments of the orchestra laid out on the stage. Music Appreciation. That was the theme. I loved music, and I loved instruments.

At one point the teacher in charge asked if anyone knew the difference between a fiddle and a violin. Well, I did, so I raised my hand. From my adult perspective, I think it was intended as a rhetorical question, but I raised my hand—the only person to do so. The teacher spotted my hand and called on me in front of the fifth, sixth, seventh, and eighth grade students in the district.

With great, pride I stood up and—in my mind, I was thinking about the difference between a violin and a bass fiddle—went into great detail explaining how a violin and a bass fiddle were alike and how they were different. I felt proud as I sat down.

The teacher had his own agenda and, by the time my little butt hit the bleacher, he had the entire assembly laughing at my answer. The point he was trying to make was that there is no real difference; the difference simply has to do with the kind of music that is being played. Classical music is played on a "violin" and country and western music is played on a "fiddle." I was mortified!

Again, decades later and with years of therapy, I realized that I had made a second life resolution that day. "Don't ever tell anyone what you think, because if you do, they will laugh at you!"

As a boy, there were three things that I loved: school, music, and sports. Not only was I the smallest boy in my class until the seventh grade, I wasn't athletic at all. I went to tryouts and was drafted – or so I thought - on one of the teams. I remember being so excited when I got my uniform that I put it on and slept in it that night. What I didn't realize until years later was that I wasn't good enough to play little league. I had not been drafted, but relegated to the "minor league" of little league. As a player, I had a reputation of "swinging at the bad ones, and letting the good ones go by." I was put out in right field, and everyone, except me, hoped the ball wouldn't come my way.

Decades later I happened to connect with my coach from those days. It was one of those conversations in which you put yourself down and hope the other person will lift you up. I commented that I must have been the worst player he had ever coached, and without a beat, he replied that I wasn't **the worst** player he ever tried to coach: I was **the next to worst player**. He then went on to name that boy.

At recess in school, when the self-appointed captains would choose up sides, not only was I the last one chosen, but there would inevitably be an argument over who **had to** take me.

I used all those experiences of the school burning, the school assembly, and the countless times of being the last one chosen to create a significant case of poor self-esteem!

As an adult, I developed what the psychologists call "Imposter Syndrome." I was successful professionally, but inwardly lived with a chronic fear that people might find out what I was really like, and not like me. I felt like a phony and I spent tremendous amounts of energy trying to pretend that I was okay, despite how I felt about myself inwardly.

Fast forward to my late sixties. I was scrolling through Facebook and came across an ad for the "Oh My Goddard! Sprint Triathlon." Prior to that, the only triathlon I knew about was the Hawaii Ironman. So I did some research and learned that there are three categories of triathlons: the Ironman (2.4 mile swim, a 112 mile bike, and a 26.2 mile run), the Olympic (just under a mile swim, a 25 mile bike, and a 6.2 mile run), and a Sprint (just under a half-mile swim, a 12 mile bike, and a 3.2 mile run).

Well, I know how to swim, I have a bike, and I have a pair of sneakers. This seemed doable to me and I had six months to train. So, I signed up!

I was so naïve, and Fate, or coincidence, or something was watching over me. I ran into a friend whom I hadn't seen for years. We were catching up and I told him about signing up for the triathlon, only to learn that he had participated in this event the year before. He strongly recommended that I sign up for the accompanying clinics. So, I did; I signed up for the package of all three: the swim, the bike, and the running clinics.

In the Swim Clinic I learned that I would need to buy a wetsuit, a special one for swimmers; it wasn't cheap! I also learned that, because the rubber is so thin, allowing flexibility for swimming, it is difficult to put on and it is easy to tear! This, I discovered, as I put my fingers through the material the very first time I tried mine on! By the time I suited up for the actual event, my wet suit looked like something resembling swiss cheese!

It was during the first ocean swim clinic that I had my first full-fledged panic attack. Open water swimming is very different from pool swimming! There is no black line on the bottom of the ocean to follow. Physically, there was no reason for my panic; I had been routinely swimming a mile in the pool, but psychologically I was in way over my head when it came to ocean swimming. Ironically, I wasn't in over my head; the tide was low, and I could have stood up to touch the bottom. It was a "head thing." Who was I, with a history of being rejected as an athlete, to think that I could accomplish a triathlon?

Fortunately, the woman running the clinic got in my face and yelled at me: "You are a triathlete! You know how to swim...so SWIM!"

WOW! Me—a triathlete! That was a label that had never been a part of my identity. It was an empowering moment!

When I showed up at the Bike Clinic, the instructor pointed out that I had a hybrid bike. I already knew that, but she told me I wouldn't want to use that for a triathlon. I would need a road bike. The cost of my foray into this triathlon was rapidly mounting.

At the Run Clinic I was told that I needed to go to a store specializing in running shoes; my sneakers would be a liability. When I was getting fitted for my new running shoes, the clerk looked at my feet and asked, "Are those technical socks?" I looked at my feet and thought, *Technically, they are socks.* I had no idea what was being asked. That's when I learned that I didn't even have the right socks to do a triathlon.

During this time of preparation, I gave myself a case of mononucleosis. (Our minds are so powerful!) This was a way of protecting my fragile ego; I reasoned that if I didn't do well, I had a legitimate excuse! This, of course, was all on an unconscious level.

But I did complete the triathlon, and later learned that I was the oldest participant that day!

Completing the triathlon was an amazing accomplishment for me, and that got me thinking about other possibilities.

Several times in my channel surfing, I had come across telecasts of Spartan Races. These are races over very difficult terrain with ridiculous obstacles. Like triathlons, there are three levels of Spartans: the Beast, which is 14+ miles and 30+ obstacles, the Super, which is 8+ miles and 25+ obstacles, and the Sprint with 3+ miles and 20+ obstacles.

During the months I started training for the triathlon, I also began attending classes with my wife at a cardio kickboxing gym. I was intrigued and I knew that the woman who owned the gym had competed in several Spartan events. One day, after kickboxing class, I sat down with her and asked if she thought I might be able to do a Spartan Race. Her eyes lit up and she exclaimed, "YES! and here's the plan: You're going to do the Beast in April, the Super in August, and in November, you'll celebrate your seventieth birthday at Fenway Park doing a Sprint, completing your Spartan Trifecta" (all three distances in the same calendar year)!

Honestly, I cringed inside! I wasn't prepared to *DO* a Spartan event. I was just asking if she thought it might be *possible*. It was an idea that was fun to think about. Actually doing it was a whole other matter!

She said, "I'm going to train you, and you are going to do this!"

Well, I did complete the Beast in April, but not without having my second ever full-fledged panic attack the night before. There were over forty people from our gym who had traveled to New Jersey to take on this challenge, and I was old enough to be the father of most of them! What was I thinking? Who did I think I was to undertake a physical trial like this?

The next morning, I discovered that just to get to the starting line, I had to climb over a four-foot wall. It took me in excess of ten hours to conquer this Beast: almost seventeen miles of very challenging terrain, with more than five thousand feet of vertical climb, all the while negotiating thirty-five ridiculous obstacles! When I jumped the line of fire at the finish line, I went off by myself and cried like a baby. I had done it! This time I didn't care who saw me cry. These were tears of joy, of pride, and of exhaustion. I accomplished something far beyond anything I had ever imagined for myself. I later learned that, like the triathlon, I was the oldest participant in the event.

The following spring, I entered my second triathlon. In the world of triathletes, you are grouped according to the age you will be on December 31st of that year, which meant that, even though I wouldn't be seventy until November, I was competing in the age group of "seventy and above." I finished first in my age group and, because of that, was invited by the U.S. Triathlon Association to try out to represent the United States in the world age-group competition in Rotterdam later that year.

Because the date conflicted with a previous commitment, I did not go to the tryouts, but instead completed a Spartan Super event and was again the oldest finisher. Then, five days after my seventieth birthday, I completed the Spartan Sprint at Fenway Park in Boston, earning my Spartan Trifecta!

Words cannot describe the feelings of accomplishment. My sense of self-esteem skyrocketed.

The lesson for me is two-fold:

1) We each have what I call an "Inner Magnificence." For me, this is a spiritual concept, but because religion stirs up emotional baggage, for the most part I choose not to use spiritual terms. This Inner Magnificence is the repository and source of our true potential, our best selves in every respect.

2) Many of us need to have someone else believe in us before we can begin to believe in ourselves. We need to have a coach or trainer or mentor who sees our potential, and who creates a plan and who holds us accountable until we finally claim our own Inner Magnificence, the part of us that was always there, but had gotten covered up by so many painful life experiences.

This is my story. This is the story behind my passion for helping others move into their **Inner Magnificence** and live the life of their potential, instead of a life shaped by fears and insecurities!

What I've discovered is that you don't have to accomplish monumental goals, like completing a triathlon or a Spartan event. You can connect with your Inner Magnificence every day by doing little things.

What follows is a series of 101 invitations. Each is a story with an invitation to action and each comes with a guarantee.

I invite you to read on and accept my invitations! The extent to which you do is the extent to which you will be able to say, "I feel good about being me!" I guarantee it!

Time Marches On

Adulting

I am amused by the number of folks who post something on Facebook to the effect that they are tired of adulting. I'm fairly certain that those same people wouldn't be willing to give up their "adult beverages."

Here's the surprise: thinking this way is a good beginning! Jesus, the master teacher, is recorded as saying, "Truly I tell you, unless you change and become like little children, you will never enter the kingdom of heaven."

We aren't supposed to live our lives adulting; we're created to live our lives playing—enjoying ourselves. We are created to see life the way little children do: free of worry with every day being a new beginning, a clean slate.

I know, you're going to start thinking about all the things you need to do: pay bills on time, go to work, take care of the kids (or your parents), get the kids to soccer practice, dance lessons, or little league practices. The list can seem almost endless, and exhausting.

One of my favorite psychology text books is *I Never Knew I Had a Choice*, by Gerald and Marianne Corey. The underlying invitation is to stop going through life, fulfilling one obligation after another, until we can finally retire and do whatever we want whenever we want. Instead, the book is an invitation to live life the way we choose to, living from a sense of joy instead of trapped by a sense of what is expected by those around us.

The greatest choice we have is in how we choose to think about life. Instead of seeing ourselves trapped by obligations, we can acknowledge that the reason we fulfill these "obligations" is because it makes us feel better about ourselves.

Here's a simple example: Most nights my wife works later than I do and most nights I try to have dinner prepared when she gets home. I could see this as an obligation; this is what a good husband should do! Or I can see it as a gift. It makes me feel good to express my love and appreciation for all she does by having dinner ready for her when she gets home.

There is a world of difference between acting from a sense of obligation and doing the same thing from a place of giving, a place of expressing gratitude.

When we're complaining about adulting, what we're really complaining about is our mental attitude. We have an Inner Magnificence that invites us to be joyful and playful, free from worry and obligation. We are created to love life, not dread Mondays. We are created to be "childlike." Caution: this does not mean "childish!" There is a significant difference! Childlike is when we live from a place of joy; childish is when we live from a place of self-absorption.

Here is my radical invitation: **If you are doing something and you can't find joy in it—then quit! Be creative and be honest. Move into your Magnificence. Choose to think about what you are doing with joy, and if you honestly can't find joy in what you're doing, then that's the Magnificent part of you telling you it's time to change what you are doing.**

Here's one caveat: Being childish doesn't serve you, but being childlike is heavenly. If you don't believe me, just ask Jesus!

The extent to which you accept my invitation is the extent to which you'll be able to say, "I feel good about being me!"

An Adventure

While in southern California, I was waiting in the limo while my colleague finished an interview, and I began talking with the driver. She's been doing this job for over five years and loves it. She told me that she used to work in an office but got tired of that and quit for a while.

When she was ready to go back to work, she knew somebody who knew somebody that had a connection with this limo company and learned that they were always looking for new drivers. I asked her how she liked it. She smiled and said, "I love it."

I went on to ask what she loved about her job.

She told me that every day is different. She meets interesting people. She gets to see parts of the area where she otherwise wouldn't go.

She is based in Santa Barbara, but goes to Los Angeles, San Francisco, Hollywood, and places all around. Sometimes on her days off, she goes back to spend time in places she had discovered because of her passengers' destinations.

I asked her about her days off and the hours she worked. She said she never knows from one day to another what her schedule might be. She said that "every day is an adventure." Sometimes she might need to start work at 1 am and sometimes she might work until 1 am. She might begin her day, and all she has is a two-hour trip, and sometimes by the end of that time, there would be another assignment.

"Every day is an adventure!" she repeated.

Wow! I don't know very many people who get up every morning and see an adventure in store.

Admittedly, she is single and can have a job with lots of unknowns in terms of schedule, but I realized that so often as I go through my day, I end up going places and doing things that I hadn't planned. Unexpected events and circumstances arise which require my time and attention.

My conversation with her was a great reminder that our attitude isn't determined by the events of our day, it is determined by how we think about our day.

What would it be like to wake up every morning and think, "I wonder what adventure I'm going to have today?" What if, instead of reacting negatively when our day takes an unexpected turn, we simply saw our whole day as an adventure?

What if we moved into our Magnificence and decided to control our attitude instead of being frustrated by all those unexpected demands and diversions?

So, here's my invitation: **When you get up tomorrow morning, be curious about the adventure you are about to experience. Do it again the next day, and the one after that—for as long as you live!**

The extent to which you accept my invitation is the extent to which you'll be able to say, "I feel good about being me!"…and that's a promise!

The Best Laid Plans

I turned in my last set of final grades. Classes won't start again for me until after Labor Day. My wife and I had a conversation about what we wanted to do with the summer. What we both realized is that unless we schedule time, unless we put our intentions on the calendar, the summer will be gone, and we will wonder what happened to it.

Time marches on, as the saying goes. It stops for no one, and it certainly doesn't go backwards. The question is how do we spend it? Do we let it go day after day? Do we talk about what we want to do someday? Or, do we plan?

That block of time between Memorial Day and Labor Day, the time we think of as summer: what are we going to do with it?

What we decided to do is to make a list of all the things we wanted to do, and then got out the calendar and scheduled them. We made some appointments with ourselves to do the things we enjoy. We took the ferry to Block Island one day and another day we went to Mark Twain's home. We didn't want to get to the end of the summer and wonder what happened.

Life is the same way. So often, we talk about the things that we'd like to do "someday," but there is no "someday" on the calendar. Then one day we wake up...and summer's over...and we still have the same list of the things we were going to do someday.

One of the habits all successful people have in common is that they make plans; they set goals and write deadlines on their calendars. What they don't do is let life set their agenda. They create their own agenda and make things happen, rather than hoping things happen.

How about you? What's on your calendar...for today...for this weekend...for this summer...for...the rest of your life?

Thanks to the movie of the same name, we are familiar with the concept of having a "Bucket List." But having a list isn't enough. It is the goal setting, it is the decision making, it is the planning, it is setting a deadline, it is putting it on the calendar that make a difference.

We each have an Inner Magnificence that gives us dreams and programs us to have rich and full lives, but to do that, we must consciously choose to take action.

So, here's my invitation: **Move into your Magnificence and, if you don't already have a Bucket List, make one; write it down. Then, get out your calendar and begin to make a date with yourself to have the experience.** It can be something as small as checking out a local nature preserve, or something as big as a trip to the Galapagos Islands, or countless experiences in between.

What matters is not that we have dreams. What matters is that we set a goal and make a plan and follow through!

The extent to which you do is the extent to which you'll be able to say, "I feel good about being me!"...and that's a promise!

Counting Down

I was talking with a teacher friend of mine the other day and asked how many days left before her summer vacation started. Her response surprised me: "I have no idea!" she said. "I love my job and I enjoy every day! I don't want to live my life counting down anything."

That got me to thinking about how we count time. My first recollection of this was when I was young, and I couldn't wait until I was old enough to start school. Then, I'm sure that when I was in school, there were times when I counted down the days before school ended and summer vacation began. I know that some of my students count down the minutes before I dismiss class. I counted the years before I was old enough to get my driver's license. Some of us counted the time before we were old enough to vote or old enough to legally buy alcohol. Some of us are counting down the years before we are old enough to retire. I know parents that are counting down the time before their children finally move out.

On the flip side, I'm at the age that, when people ask, I find myself telling them how old I'm going to be on my next birthday. I also am experiencing the phenomenon that so many of my elders talked about: how quickly time goes by the older we get.

I am now in what Erik Erikson called the "Older Adult" stage of life, the stage when we become keenly aware that the number of days ahead of us is far fewer than the number of days behind us. Knowing this, I find myself increasingly asking, "Is what I'm doing right now worthy of my time and energy? Is this how I want to spend THIS DAY of my life?"

In conversations, I often hear people say something to the effect of, "I'd love to, but I just don't have the time." The more honest statement is, "It's simply not important enough for me to spend my time doing it." (Note: It is probably better to just know this than it is to say it out loud!)

How about you? How are you spending your time? Are you enjoying what you are doing? Are you savoring the moment? Are you using time wisely? Are you passing time? Are you counting down the days until…?

We each have an Inner Magnificence that invites us to a life of meaning.

So, here's my invitation: **No matter where you are in life, find a way to make each day count, whatever that might mean to you. Maybe it is appreciating the beauty around you, maybe it is enjoying some of life's pleasures, maybe it is making a difference for another person, or maybe it is challenging yourself to experience something you've never done before.**

The extent to which you do is the extent to which you'll be able to say, "I feel good about being me!"…and that's a promise!

Evolution of...Air and Space

I t had been decades since I last visited the Smithsonian Air and Space Museum in Washington, D.C. Just as I remembered, it was an awe-inspiring presentation of the evolution of flying. As my wife and I walked through the museum, I noticed two trends: 1) how air travel has evolved and changed through the years, and 2) how we have taken our technology of flying and converted it into increasingly sophisticated ways of killing people.

Sometimes in my more philosophical moods, I think about war and how in our earliest history, when we were angry, we struck people with our hands and fists, then we probably used clubs, which evolved into spears. From there, we made bows and arrows, all the while creating more distance between us and our opponent, yet continuing the lethal nature of our interaction.

Next, we combined black powder and lead and created guns, so we could kill people from even farther away. We devised ways to make guns bigger and we manufactured cannons. We took the concept of explosive devices and, with the advent of airplanes, realized that we can drop bombs from the sky, killing people and destroying property.

9

As our technology continued to develop, we developed guided missiles and "smart bombs." Airplanes became a delivery system for weapons. Now, we have unmanned drones that can be flown by people safely ensconced in front of a computer screen thousands of miles away.

All the while, we are making flying safer and more efficient for everyday travel. We have made the world smaller and foreign places much more accessible. I guess this is a good example as to how technology is neither good nor bad; it depends on how it is used.

I am thinking about the old spiritual, "Ain't Gonna Study War no More!" I am thinking about the passages from the Old Testament prophets Isaiah and Micah about "beating swords into plowshares and spears into pruning hooks." I'm thinking about the power of Gandhi's non-violent approach returning India to a self-governing country.

What I would love would be a museum dedicated to the evolution of how we have learned to live together peaceably, a collection of creative solutions to conflicts between individuals, groups, and nations.

My contention is that every one of us has an Inner Magnificence, even though we may not act from that place. While I DO understand that there is some sense of gratification and satisfaction when we exact revenge on those who threaten us or treat us badly, our Magnificence gets expressed to the extent that we recognize human connections and, instead of inflicting damage, we choose to put energy into understanding. Our Magnificence gets expressed when, instead of judging, we act from love rather than fear.

So, here's my invitation: **the next time you feel threatened or hurt, take a second and think about the loving response. Be creative. Tune into a response that comes from your Inner Magnificence. Make peace, not war.**

The extent to which you do will be the extent to which you'll be able to say, "I feel good about being me!"...and that's a promise.

Face-plant

I had an incident while traveling. I did a face-plant on the tile floor of the motel where my wife and I were staying. The alarm was set for 3:30 am because we had a 6 am flight to catch. I didn't sleep well, feeling anxious about getting up on time, catching the taxi, and getting through the TSA check point on time.

I remember going to the bathroom, then heading back out to get dressed. The next thing I knew I heard my wife calling my name and her hand was rubbing my back. "Wake up! You're bleeding!" she said. Sure enough, I opened my eyes and, picking my head off the floor, saw small puddles of blood dripping from my nose. I couldn't figure out what happened. One minute, I'm leaving the bathroom to get dressed, and the next minute I'm on the floor with a bloody nose.

My mind was foggy at first, trying to figure out what happened. It took me a while, but I realized that it all was because of the side effects of some medication I take at night for my restless leg syndrome. I got up quickly and was moving with too much of a sense of urgency, then BOOM! I'm totally unconscious.

An interesting fact is that the only way we know we've been asleep is because we wake up! We never are aware of that moment when we go from feeling drowsy to being asleep. It took my wife calling my name and rubbing my back to pull me out of my unconscious state. It was a literal "Wake up!" call.

This got me to think about other ways we seem to be living our lives, hurrying from one commitment to another, feverishly checking things off on our to-do list. Then the next thing we know, we're on the floor with a bloody nose, wondering what happened.

Life can do that to us. For one reason or another, we simply go "unconscious" for a while. It may only be for a very short time, or it may be much longer. Life passes by, and suddenly, we realize that, while we have no recollection of how we got to where we are, we do know that it isn't where we want to be.

Sometimes we are fortunate enough to have a person in our life who cares enough to call us out, to invite us to come back into consciousness, to get up off the floor, to figure out what is going on, and then move forward with intention and purpose. Other times, we are by ourselves when we wake up and wonder how we ended up flat on our faces, maybe even with a bloody nose.

Often what I think is that we get going too fast; we feel so much pressure to be somewhere, to do something, and without even realizing it, we do a face-plant.

So, here's my invitation: **If you do discover that you've done a face-plant with life, move into your Magnificence. Pick yourself up and reorient yourself. Slow down and be in the moment; trust that everything will work out one way or another. It always does!**

The extent to which you accept my invitation is the extent to which you'll be able to say, "I feel good about being me!"...and that's a promise!

Take Ten!

B ack in the late 1990s, a couple of psychoanalysts wrote a book called *The Fifty Minute Hour*, and told the story of five clinical case studies. Even before then, the term "fifty-minute hour" was used, with some derision as I recall, to describe the length of a standard therapy session. This was before managed care took over and dictated the length of therapy sessions.

The concept implied that the client was paying for an hour-long session, but only getting fifty minutes. In fact, the clinician was using the "extra" ten minutes to write notes, go to the bathroom, get a cup of coffee, make phone calls, etc., to recharge their emotional and physical batteries before beginning the next session.

I have recently acquired a new appreciation for the fifty-minute hour, not as a therapist, but as a person who spends a fair amount of time working at my desk. I got the concept from Brendon Burchard on one of his podcasts. His research suggests that when we have a heavy work load, we do better work and we do it more efficiently when we take regular breaks. Instead of doing what I usually try to do: power through, and "get 'r done!"

It turns out that, by taking regular breaks, getting up, moving around, and perhaps drinking a glass of water, we end up getting more done. Research also shows that the quality is better, and here's the real surprise, we have more energy at the end of our day! How's that for a recipe for success? It goes back to that old saying of "Work smarter, not harder!" Who would have guessed that the smarter way to work is by using a fifty-minute hour?

Some of us pride ourselves in our ability to work hard and there **is** great satisfaction in putting in a hard day's work and seeing what we've accomplished. Research shows that by taking regular breaks, we can still get a lot done, and feel refreshed instead of tired.

So, back to those psychiatrists who only allowed their clients fifty minutes, even though they billed for the entire hour. The reality is that those patients got more of the clinician's energy and attention and ultimately, better therapy, because of that ten extra minutes they afforded themselves between each session.

The same is true for us: whatever it is that needs our full attention, whatever the project is that requires lots of work, give yourself, and the project, your best by honoring the fifty-minute hour.

So, here's my invitation: **move into your Magnificence and the next time you have a big project, set the timer on your phone for fifty minutes, and when the alarm goes off, take ten!**

At the end of the day, you'll be glad you did. You'll also be able to say, "I feel good about being me!"…and that's a promise!

A Grave Observation

I have what some might call a morbid attraction to cemeteries. I like spending time reading the headstones. Sadly, many of the old epitaphs have been eaten away by the ravages of acid rain and time itself. I think that's a shame, because many of them contained gems of wisdom or interesting capsules of the person's life.

This past weekend, I was attracted to the cemetery on Block Island, RI. As I looked at the various plots of the families who originally bought the island, I was struck by the way the ages were engraved on the headstones.

Overall, the folks buried there didn't live as long as our expected life times. One was born and died on the same day. An occasional soul lived into their ninth decade. There were many children, which always feels sad to me. I can't imagine losing a child, and I hope that is one of life's experiences that I am spared.

What did strike me is the way people of earlier generations recorded their ages: two years, four months, and twenty-three days; seventy-nine years, eleven months, and twelve days; thirty-eight years, six months, and seventeen days. Today, we tend to think about our age in terms of years.

Sure, months count when we think about the size of clothes for newborns: 0-3 months, 3-6 months, etc. Sometimes we can find clothes for a toddler up to twenty-four months. After that we think in terms of height and weight, not months.

Children often describe themselves in terms of half-years, as in "I'm four and a half!" but the rest of us count our years. I suspect some of that has to do with legislation using age as defining life's privileges: the age at which we can get our driver's license, the age that we can legally vote or purchase alcohol, retirement age, or the age when we are eligible for Social Security and Medicare. These are all determined by our age in years, but those weren't issues for our forebearers.

As we have focused on our years, we have forgotten our days. I am reminded of the Old Testament passage from Psalms: *Teach us to number our days aright, that we may gain a heart of wisdom.*

As I walked through the cemetery and read the ages, exact to the day, I realized that it was a call, a reminder, an invitation for all who see the inscriptions to ask ourselves, "What are we doing to make our days count?" Do we value each day, or do our days get lost in years?

Am I living with the goal of having my name announced on a TV or radio program as one who has marked the centennial of my birth, or is my goal something more?

We each have an Inner Magnificence that wants more for us.

So, here's my invitation: ***Resolve to make each day count!* Find a way to allow your Magnificence to shine, every day, for as many years, months, and days as you have!**

The extent to which you do is the extent to which you'll be able to say, "I feel good about being me!"…and that's a promise!

Ikigai, My Raison D'être

Dan Beuttner has done extensive research for *National Geographic* on what he calls the "Blue Zones." These are places on earth where people live longer and remain healthier. He found four places on the globe where this happens, and he then studied these places to look for common threads.

It turns out that one of the common denominators is a concept called "ikigai," a Japanese word that roughly translates as "reason for being." Our culture doesn't have a corresponding word, but the concept has to do with why we get out of bed in the morning, and it isn't because our bladder is full. Neither does it have to do with any sense of obligation, like going to work or getting the kids off to school. It has more to do with service, with what gives meaning to your life. It has to do with opportunities to which you are looking forward. It is the reason we're glad to get out of bed and start our day.

The key is not why you *have to* get out of bed every morning, but why do you *want to* get out of bed. What is the contribution you are looking forward to making in the lives of others, be it family, friends, or the world in general?

What is it that makes you smile? What is it that you feel passionately about? What cause have you committed yourself to supporting?

I realize that sometimes we do need to focus on ourselves and our needs, but science and spirituality both tell us that for life to be rich and meaningful, for life to be joyous and long, we would do well to be invested in a cause bigger than ourselves.

We have an Inner Magnificence and, when we live from that place, we act in ways that make this world a better place. It might be something as simple as taking care of our grandchildren. Maybe it is being the janitor at an elementary school. It doesn't have to be anything grandiose, but it has to involve giving ourselves. Some people's contribution might be worthy of a Nobel Prize, and another's contribution might go unnoticed by almost everyone. What matters doesn't have anything to do with what our reason is to get out of bed; what matters is that we have one bigger than ourselves!

There is scientific evidence that without this sense of purpose, we compromise our health and we shorten our lives by as much as seven years.

You may already know yours and be living for it, but what I've discovered is that most of us have a limited vision, thinking that the reason to get out of bed is to go to work, and many of us look forward to the day we can retire and sleep as long as we want.

So, here's my invitation: **Find your ikigai! If you don't already know what it is, begin to play with this idea. Be curious about what it might be that would cause you to be eager to start your day, because you know that you're going to make a difference either in someone's life, or in the well-being of the planet.**

The extent to which you claim yours is the extent to which you'll be able to say, "I feel good about being me!"…and that's a promise!

In the Moment

She was five, waiting outside for the bus to come take her to kindergarten. She was truly experiencing the moment. "Mom, do you smell that?"

"What do you smell?" her mother asked.

"Just an ordinary, awesome day!" she said.

Just an ordinary, awesome day! How often do YOU smell that?

Contrast that with me the other day, intent on getting things done, knocking off one thing after another on my to-do list. I stopped at the gas station to get the tank filled then went to the carwash to get rid of an accumulation of pollen and bird droppings. Then I was headed home to sit down and write.

To my horror, as I pulled out of the carwash, I looked in the driver's side mirror and saw that, not only had I left the panel cover open, I had also left the gas cap dangling below. Yes, it was a carwash that had powerful jets of water, spraying detergent, wax, and rinse water. How could I have possibly been so careless as to drive away from the gas pump, leaving the gas cap off and the panel open? The answer is simple: because I wasn't paying attention to what I was doing. I was preoccupied with what I was going to do next!

I got home in a panic and desperately poured a bottle of a solution that is supposed to remove water from your gasoline, hoping I hadn't done damage to my fuel system. Fortunately, it seems the treatment worked. I've gone through a couple of tanks of gas since with seemingly no problems.

I shudder to think what could have happened, all because I wasn't thinking about what I was doing, all because I wasn't truly present in the moment.

I now wonder what else I miss by not being in the moment. I suspect I miss a lot of the beauty of the world because, instead of soaking in the moment, I'm focused on things I need to be doing.

We've all heard horror stories, from something as big as forgetting to pick up your child after school or from daycare, to something as little as putting a cup of coffee on the roof while you load the car and then driving away, with your coffee spilling all over your roof and maybe even the car behind you. Have you ever put something in the microwave, only to open it several hours later and realize that you forgot that you put it there? I suspect we are all guilty of things like this on one occasion or another.

From time to time, life gives us reminders, sometimes gentle and sometimes dramatic, that life is better lived when we are fully present, in the moment, even when we are just waiting for the bus or filling our gas tank.

We have an Inner Magnificence that wants us to have a joyful life and it knows that the best strategy is for us to be completely in the moment, completely in the present, not ruminating over past grievances or mistakes, not thinking about what we need to be doing next, not distracting ourselves by multi-tasking, but simply being fully present in the moment.

Here's my invitation: **Make a conscious decision that, whatever you are doing, you are going to pay attention to every detail; immerse yourself fully in the present. Choose to savor every moment of this ordinary awesome day!**

The extent to which you do is the extent to which you'll be able to say, "I feel good about being me!"…and that's a promise!

20

Inner Voice

I had already removed the cover and was about to unscrew the wires on a light switch that had gone bad in the kitchen. Suddenly, something told me to get a simple circuit tester and be sure the power was off.

This was a silly thought! I had already gone to the basement and started flipping breakers in the panel box, asking my wife to tell me when the power went off in the kitchen. She did, and I began to replace the faulty switch. I had already disconnected the power from the kitchen: what was the need to check? Nothing else was working. But I did check and—surprise, surprise—that box was "hot." Everything else in the kitchen was dead, with the sole exception of this one fixture.

This was a wonderful reminder to pay attention to that little voice that sometimes suggests a behavior that doesn't make sense in the moment. Some call it intuition, others call it Divine Guidance, yet others call it that "still, small voice." Whatever you call it, it's the voice that, when I pay attention to it, I'm almost *always* glad I did. And, when I don't, I almost always regret it.

I can tell you lots of times when I didn't pay attention. Once, I was prompted to see a friend in the hospital. I had seen him the day before. The voice said, "Go now!" but "now" wasn't convenient, and my plan was to see him later in the day. When I did go, at a "convenient time," I walked in to an empty room. My friend's body had just been removed and taken to the morgue!

Years ago I was walking across campus and saw a friend sitting on a rock, holding what looked like a letter. Instead of speaking to her, as I normally would, I was led to walk over and sit down beside her, saying nothing. We sat there in silence for what seemed like an eternity (it was probably less than fifteen or twenty minutes). I sensed something profound was happening in the silence. All I knew was that the air full of powerful feelings. Then the feeling lightened. She turned to me, smiled, and as she got up and started to walk away, she said, "Thank you!"

In all the years later, neither one of us ever referred to that afternoon. To this day, I have no idea what was in that letter she was holding. I only knew that I was drawn to share my physical presence and join her in silence. I've since lost contact, but have never forgotten that afternoon.

We have this amazing Inner Magnificence that somehow has access to information well beyond what our five senses tell us. We have access to information in ways that we have yet to understand. Sometimes the information comes as an insight, a solution to a problem we've been struggling with for the longest time. More often it comes to us as an invitation to act, to do something specific. It often doesn't make sense. Sometimes it calls us to act "out of character." It comes as a gentle prompting.

Whatever you call it, here's the invitation: **Pay attention to it!**

The extent to which you do is the extent to which you'll be able to say, "I feel good about being me!"…and that's a promise!

The Journey

Every time I get behind the wheel, it is because I'm going some-place. I have a destination! Invariably, I trust the Waze app to constantly calculate the fastest way to get there. I look for the interstate highways. Usually, I'm not big on taking the side roads, no matter how much more scenic they might be. When I'm on a mission, my focus is on my destination.

Recently, I've been thinking about how this applies to my cur-rent project of writing this book composed of my blogs and I've been feeling a lot of pressure around this. I went through a time when I was disciplined during the summer and had a productive time of writing. Then school was back in session. I had a full course load, and in addition to all of that, I wanted to market myself as a speaker and trainer, a suc-cess coach and consultant. My writing took a back seat. The project of writing has felt like a heavy weight hanging over me.

One morning in my quiet time, I had one of those "Aha!" mo-ments and realized that instead of being so focused on the outcome (get-ting the book done), I would be much better served by allowing myself to enjoy the process.

I wonder how many of us are so busy trying to get somewhere, so focused on some future event when life is going to be better, that we are missing the joy of today!

If the journey isn't joyful, what's the point of going? How many of us numb our lives getting through until…? Until what? You fill in the blank. How many of us miss the joy because we are so busy trying to reach some goal?

I know a lot of people who are constantly talking about how busy they are, but I don't hear many talking about how joyful they are in their busyness.

Carmen Basilio, a middle-weight boxing champion, once said, "I loved boxing. I loved every minute of it, every round in the gym, every skip of the rope, and every foot on the road. The fights were the dessert." He didn't go through all of the training just so he could fight; he learned to enjoy every aspect of being a boxer.

Goals keep us motivated; they give us direction, but if we wait until the goal is accomplished, we miss the joy of the journey.

So, here's my invitation: **Move into your Magnificence and whatever your situation, whether you are raising a family and looking forward to the day when the kids are on their own, or working toward retirement and looking forward to that day that you wake up and can do anything you want, decide to enjoy the journey. Whether you are writing a book or paying off a college loan, whether you are being intentional about losing weight or staying clean and sober, enjoy each day. Whether you are training for an athletic competition or driving hundreds of miles to see family and friends, decide to enjoy the journey. If you can't find joy, then choose another path. Either way, you owe it to yourself to enjoy your life's journey every day!**

The extent to which you do is the extent to which you'll be able to say, "I feel good about being me!"…and that's a promise.

Imagine That!

I just returned from spending a delightful weekend with my three youngest grandsons, ages six, five, and almost four. My wife couldn't go but, because I was going to be there over St. Patrick's Day, she sent a book called *How to Catch a Leprechaun*. The story tells about the mischief a leprechaun made at school and the ensuing mess. It ended with a challenge for the students to set a trap and stop his mischief.

After reading the book with my grandsons, we decided to set some of our own leprechaun traps around the house, just in case. We spent hours scheming and planning and experimenting with various designs for traps.

Afterwards, there was great excitement as we checked the traps regularly. Though we didn't catch any, we did discover that one had evidently taken some of our bait and exchanged it for gold coins made of chocolate.

As I was cleaning up after supper that evening, the littlest guy grabbed my leg and, with tears in his eyes, admitted that he was afraid of leprechauns. I assured him that no leprechaun has ever in the history of the universe hurt anyone. I guaranteed him that leprechauns were happy funny and just liked to play tricks.

I thought I put his fears to rest, but when his mother got home later that evening, he told her how afraid he was. She handled the situation much better, by telling him that there really is no such thing as leprechauns, and that they are only imaginary. With great relief, he announced to his older brothers that there are no such things as leprechauns and that, "PopPop had played a trick on us!" The older brothers promptly refuted him, reminding him that, "PopPop was with us the WHOLE time, and couldn't possible have switched the bait!"

The good thing is that, by bedtime, everyone was satisfied with their own version of the truth. Despite being imaginary, the leprechaun left even more chocolate coins to be discovered near the traps the next morning.

The story illustrates the power of our imagination and how we believe the things that we want to be true and how we scare ourselves with things that aren't true. The older boys wanted to continue to believe, because it was fun when they were looking for chocolate coins. The little guy wanted to believe the leprechaun was me, because that made the whole idea feel much less threatening.

What about you? Does your imagination work for you, or against you?

Do you allow your imagination to create images that are fun to play with, or are your images more of the scary variety? Do we get stuck in the literal, or can we play with the imaginary?

It is sort of like Santa Claus. Does he really exist? Literally, no, and just the thought of him can be scary for some children. (I know, because I was one of them!) But the idea of gifts that come from the sky (so to speak) is fun to think about and, as adults, to embody.

Here's my invitation for you: **Give permission to the imagination of your Inner Magnificence to have fun, to be playful, and to take on the spirit of the leprechauns. And, when scary thoughts begin to creep in, remind yourself that there is superficial truth and there is deep Truth and that Truth always reflects joy and goodness and light and love!**

The extent to which you know this is the extent to which you'll be able to say, "I feel good about being me!"…and that's a promise!

There's an App for That

One semester my teaching schedule had me ending a class at Bryant University at 3:15 pm in Smithfield, RI and beginning my next class at 3:50 pm at Johnson and Wales University in downtown Providence, RI. This is approximately a fifteen-mile trip. That does not include the time it takes me to walk from my Bryant classroom to the parking lot, nor the time it takes me to find a parking spot and walk to my classroom "Down City," as it is sometimes called.

This is where Waze comes in. For those of you who don't know, Waze is an app that gives directions from where you are to where you are going and it calculates the quickest route in real time, meaning that it "knows" the current traffic conditions and takes that into consideration as it plots out the route.

On any given day, it might give me completely different directions to get to my next destination. I have discovered more back alleys and little cut throughs than I ever would have imagined or explored on my own. The technology is amazing!

So, I was thinking about what a great invention it would be to have a sort of "Waze" for life. You know, some sort of inner software program that, once I decide where I want my life to go, it would guide me around the road

27

blocks and obstacles, helping me get where I want to go in life with less hassle and frustration and disappointment.

As enchanted as I was with the concept, the more I thought about it, the more I realized the wisdom in NOT having access to such programing.

The purpose of Waze is to help us get from one place to another as efficiently as possible.

The purpose of life is NOT NECESSARILY for us to get from where we are to where we want to be with the same efficiency.

As I see it, life is not about efficiency; life is about growth and meaning. Sometimes where we think we want to go isn't really in our overall best interest. Sometimes life has a wisdom of its own and seems to put up obstacles to help us see that there is a better destination. We have an Inner Magnificence that knows about a destination that has much more meaning, a destination that will give a much deeper sense of fulfillment, but we wouldn't have known that without getting past the obstacle and the consequent detour.

Instead of our goal being to get through life as effortlessly as possible, what if our goal was to have a life of adventure, of growth, of experiences that give richness and depth? What if, instead of avoiding the unpleasantness, we saw the frustrations as opportunities to grow and evolve a life that has substance? What if we chose to see every frustration as an opportunity to make our lives bigger? What if we saw every difficulty, not as something to avoid, but as an opportunity to discover the Inner Magnificence we are. What if life is an opportunity to discover and enjoy a deep sense of accomplishment?

So, here's my invitation: **The next time you run into a situation that was completely unexpected, instead of looking at it as a hindrance, see it as an invitation to discover and explore the amazing resources of your Inner Magnificence.**

The extent to which you do is the extent to which you'll be able to say, "I feel good about being me!"…and that's a promise!

Sometime....

As an adjunct professor, I am paid by the course and am required to sign a contract prior to the beginning of the semester. Representatives of the university and I all sign, agreeing on what I'm being asked to teach and the compensation. Also, as with most contracts, there is an abundance of fine print.

I realized on the first day of class that I didn't remember signing a contract. Wanting to be a responsible employee, I went to the Dean's Office to see if my contract was on file. I was hoping that I had taken care of it when I first received it, and then forgot about it. The folks in the office looked diligently and told me the date (weeks before) that they had sent it out. They graciously asked me to go home and look for it and, if I couldn't find it, they'd reissue my contract for all the appropriate signatures.

I looked in lots of places to no avail. Then, I saw a pile of stuff that I had put aside, thinking, *I'll deal with all of this after the holidays.* There it was: in the middle of the pile of papers on my desk!

The holidays had come and were long gone, but my pile was still there. My plan hadn't changed; I would deal with it after the holidays. The problem is that I didn't give myself a specific deadline; I just planned on doing it sometime in the future.

I want to believe that I'm not the only one who's like this. We have piles of papers that we're going to go through sometime. There are things in our lives that are out of order, and we tolerate them and assure ourselves that we'll get around to them sometime.

Maybe it is a mess in the garage. Maybe it is that box of pictures that you've had for years. Maybe it is a desk drawer full of miscellaneous odds and ends. Maybe it is a closet full of old clothes or maybe it is a pile in the basement. Some of it is worth saving and other things need to be tossed. Like me, your intentions are good. You are committed to doing something with it sometime!

What I know are three things: 1) sometimes important things get lost in the piles; 2) "sometime" isn't a date on any calendar; and 3) every time we look at our stuff, it drains us of energy. Yes, it takes energy to live with messy piles, energy that could be freed to use in creative and joyous ways.

So, here's my invitation: **Look around your living space; look at the stuff you're going to do something with "someday." Then pick a day to begin. Maybe just commit a limited amount of time, ten minutes or an hour or two, but put it on your calendar. Then pick a date by which you will finish putting your stuff in order.**

We have an Inner Magnificence that is worthy of living in an orderly environment. Admittedly, creating order out of seeming chaos isn't necessarily a fun project, and that's why it is still there. Give yourself the gift of more energy; give yourself the gift of living in a neatly organized environment.

The extent to which you accept my invitation is the extent to which you'll be spared the experience of frantically looking for something important; it is also the extent to which you'll be able to say, "I feel good about being me!"...and that's a promise!

Times Like These

He was twenty-eight, with a devoted wife and two beautiful children, ages six and four, and he had only hours, if not minutes left to live. His cancer had won the battle. I had a prayer with the family and walked out of his crowded hospital room, and was talking with a couple of his friends.

"We just have to accept God's will," one of them said.

In my arrogance, I replied, "I don't believe a loving God would 'will' that Jimmy die and leave his family like this!"

She stopped and stared into space, then said, "No, I guess I don't either, but in times like these we have to believe something!"

It isn't that we must believe something—it is that *we do* believe something. What we do believe makes all the difference in how we respond to painful and tragic experiences, experiences of great loss and sadness.

For those who believe life is random, it isn't so much of a problem. They just accept it philosophically and go on. It stinks, but "that's life!" Or maybe they accept the trite explanation: Only the good die young!

For those of us who come from a religious tradition, we were taught that God is good, and God is love. But when we stop and really think about what we were taught, sometimes the teachings are contradictory. Sometimes we fall back on society's explanations: "God needed another angel in heaven!" REALLY?

God didn't already have enough angels, so God took him and left a twenty-seven-year-old widow and two small children to fend for themselves? REALLY?

Is God loving or selfish? You can't have it both ways.

If we believe that the nature of God is Love, and if we believe that God is present everywhere, and if we believe that God is all-powerful, and if we believe that God is all-knowing, then however we explain the painful experiences in life—times like these—then we must have an explanation that takes all of our beliefs into account.

I don't know how to reconcile all of life's painful experiences with what I believe to be true of the majestic power of the universe. I can only conclude that there is more for me to learn, that there is much that I don't yet understand.

What I do believe is that we each have an Inner Magnificence which is an expression of the Magnificence of the Cosmos. What I believe is that—in times like these—there is something bigger going on than I can comprehend.

So, here's my invitation to you: **When you find yourself in "times like these," when you find yourself in the midst of a painful experience, accept the mystery and trust that—despite all outward appearances, despite how it all feels in the moment—something good is at work which is beyond your understanding.**

The extent to which you accept my invitation is the extent to which you'll move into your magnificence and connect with a sense of peace about it all; the extent to which you do is the extent that you will feel good about life and about being you…and that's a promise!

What Do You REALLY Do?

Her friends call her Mel and she teaches first grade in a parochial school. She's been doing it now for over twenty years, and when I ask her what she likes about her job, her face lights up. "There are so many things," she said. "I love when they realize they can read. It changes their lives, and I know I had a part in making that happen!" She doesn't just teach first grade, she changes lives forever by helping six-year-olds discover their potential.

Hearing her story made me think of another Mel that I had the privilege of working with decades ago in a factory that makes distribution transformers (those cans you see hanging on electric poles). We worked on an assembly line. On the surface, his job was boring and physically demanding. We built the "guts" of a transformer, the core and coil assembly. It was a dirty and physically demanding job, but when you asked him what he did, he smiled and said, "I help provide electricity for homes where families can heat and cool their houses; they can cook their food and watch TV or sit at the kitchen table with parents playing games or helping their kids do homework." That's what he thought about as he was working. This was the vision that kept him going and allowed him to enjoy coming to work every day.

How about you? What do you do? Do you have a job you love, or do you have a job that you dread going to or do you have a job where the highlight of the week is "Hump Day" because you're over half way to the weekend when you can enjoy yourself again for a couple of days before another Monday rolls around?

How we think about what we do makes a difference—both in terms of how we feel about what we do, and how well we do what we do.

Seeing the paycheck at the end of the week, or every two weeks, or every month can be enough to get us out of bed and go to work. But when we see meaning in what we do, when we KNOW that what we are doing makes a difference in people's lives—people we may know intimately and people we may never know—that's where the joy is found.

Every job I've ever had had aspects that weren't enjoyable; it comes with the territory. Even those of us who have a job that allows us to express our passion; even those jobs have their challenges, their difficult days, but we have an Inner Magnificence that is programed to give us joy, even in the midst of our work.

I'm convinced that what makes the difference between whether we experience joy or drudgery is the meaning we attach to what we do, the vision we have about the larger contribution we are making to the world and the people in it.

So, here's the invitation: **Move into your Magnificence, and whatever it is that you do, think about the big picture; think about how the lives of others are better because of the contribution you make every day. And if you can't see how you are contributing to the world around you, stop what you're doing, and get a job that does!**

The extent to which you do is the extent to which you'll be able to say, "I feel good about being me!"…and that's a promise!

Healthy Thoughts

Checkup

I saw my primary care physician for my annual physical exam. I didn't go because something was wrong. I went more because I wanted to be reassured that I am okay. The receptionist did all the usual procedures, beginning with recording my weight and BMI, blood pressure and pulse (I had one!). We talked about the meds I'm taking and how they were working.

However, before my doctor started the physical exam, she talked to me. She asked me lots of questions about what I'm doing with my time, about my family, about my hobbies and interests. She wanted to find out how I am doing emotionally, what my stress level is. She wanted to know my sources of stress and pleasure. She wanted to know how my life was, not just how my body is.

What my doctor knows is that my physical health starts with my emotional health. If we're not healthy emotionally—and I would add spiritually—the odds of us being physically healthy are slim.

As much as we talk about our health care system in this country, and there is much to talk about when people have monthly premiums of hundreds of dollars and still can't even afford the co-pays, we don't have a formalized system to offer regular checkups on our emotional wellbeing.

That's where personal responsibility comes into play. When was the last time you sat down with a professional to have an honest conversation about your emotional health? Sure, some of us are in therapy; we go to counseling, but usually that only happens *after* we begin experiencing some sort of emotional or physical crisis.

Sometimes when we have a checkup, we are reassured that everything is fine. Sometimes, we discover that we need to make some changes. For me, making the initial change is relatively easy. It is maintaining the change that is the challenge. I'm thinking now about the number of times I've resolved to eat healthier and lose weight. In times like these, what I need is someone to regularly hold me accountable.

In my counseling practice, I used to have clients that came to me initially experiencing some sort of upset in their lives. After I helped them work through to a healthier place, they wanted to continue to see me sometimes weekly or sometimes monthly, just to help them stay on track. My role was to keep them accountable with making emotionally healthy choices for themselves.

How about you? When was the last time you took time away from everything in your life and reflected on how your life is going? What is working well? What isn't? What could be better? Is how you are today setting you up to be how you want to be a year from now, or are you even thinking that far ahead? If you keep doing what you're doing, will that increase, or decrease, the odds that you'll have a happy and healthy life?

So, here's my invitation: **Move into your Magnificence. Schedule a checkup. Set aside some quiet time for yourself or see a friend that you respect or even see a professional. Do some deep self-reflecting. If you already know you need to make some changes (most of us don't need to be told, we know), find someone who will hold you accountable in a loving and supportive way.**

The extent to which you do is the extent to which you'll be able to say, "I feel good about being me!"…and that's a promise!

Count to Ten

I was talking with a friend this morning who was pointing out how someone had "keyed" the side of her son's car. She was always reminding him to make good decisions, but the other night, he went out to eat and, since the restaurant parking lot was full, he decided to park in the lot of the apartment complex next door. Evidently, one of the residents took offense and retaliated.

When her son showed her what had happened, her immediate angry reaction was something to the effect of, "You deserved it and I'm glad it happened! Now maybe you'll listen to me!"

It didn't take her long to realize that, instead of helping, her response was hurtful. To her credit, she did apologize to her son, but, as we know, once we speak anything, the words are out there, and we can't take it back. We can do damage control, but the damage has been done.

What she recognized was that it wasn't so much the words she spoke, but the timing and the tone of her words. In retrospect, it would have been more supportive to first acknowledge his hurt at having the car he loved so much be damaged intentionally by some stranger. There would be a time later to talk about what happened and the consequences of his decision.

How often have we been a part of a conversation and reacted in anger? How often has our reaction been hurtful instead of supportive?

Like my friend, it wasn't so much that her message was not helpful; it was her timing. She also could have "self-edited." She wasn't *really* glad it happened. That comment was completely unnecessary, and hurtful. There would be a time to talk to her son about his seeming unwillingness to take advantage of her life experience. There would be a time to remind him that she admonished him about his decisions because she wanted him to avoid the hurts and disappointments that were part of her life experience. But she didn't wait for that time; she reacted immediately and she reacted out of anger.

The first lesson here is to *pay attention when people with more life history speak.* Spare yourself unnecessary pain.

The second lesson is for those of us who give advice that comes from our life experience to remember that there is a time to teach and there is a time for empathy. It isn't an either-or situation. Offering empathy to someone we love who is hurting *always* comes first. Then, as the rawness of the hurt feelings begin to heal, comes the time to reinforce the lesson and the logic behind it.

Too often we get caught up in "teaching somebody a lesson," but the conversation is tainted with so much anger that our efforts only add more pain. Timing and tone are everything!

So, here's my invitation: **Remember that adage of, when we're angry, counting to ten before we speak or act. While we're counting, give ourselves and all involved the opportunity to let it be a time of healing first, and lesson-teaching afterwards.**

When we do that, we honor our own Inner Magnificence, as well as that of the other person. Every time we speak from that perspective, we give ourselves the opportunity to say, "I feel good about being me!"…and that's a promise!

Easier at Home...NOT!

Several years ago, I decided that I would be more consistent in my exercising if it were more convenient, if I didn't have to trouble myself by getting in the car and going somewhere. So, I set about collecting workout equipment, some new and some used. I set up a respectable gym in the basement. It started with a top-of-the-line Soloflex Muscle Machine. Later I added an assortment of dumbbells, a barbell, weights, and a weight bench. I was enthusiastic for a while, and then the equipment began to serve as a major dust-collector. When I moved, I ended up giving away all the weights and equipment that I couldn't sell. As good an idea as it seemed at the time, it didn't work for me. I discovered that I am much more likely to work out by going to the gym, a real gym, than by taking advantage of my gym in the basement.

Fast forward to a recent conversation with a friend who graduated from college and got a sales job, one that he could do by phone at home. He was wise enough to know that—for him at least—he needed structure and routine.

His solution was to create a schedule in which he would get up at the same time every morning, eat, shower, get dressed as if he was going to work, then be "at work" by 9 A.M. sharp, at home, with the telephone in hand. He said he needed to feel like he had a real job, not just making a bunch of phone calls from home, and he's become very successful at what he does with a real office and several employees of his own.

What I realized about myself is that I, too, need structure; I need routine, I need a schedule. So here I am at my new "office," a.k.a. the library. My "job" this summer is to finish writing this book and I've realized that, for me, trying to work from home is fraught with too many distractions. Sure, it is convenient. I can spend the whole morning in my PJs, working at the computer. However, it is easy to distract myself from writing and start doing trivial things around the house. By the time I realize it, the whole morning is gone and I have almost nothing to show for it.

We each have an Inner Magnificence that invites us to live with a sense of accomplishment, a sense of having done something that matters, something that makes a difference. There is no single "right way" to go about this; we each have our own styles.

What I know for me is that I need to separate home from work and from exercise. I need to create boundaries and structure to keep me from distracting myself from accomplishing what I say I value.

So, here's my invitation: **Ask yourself: what are the deceptions you are creating and believing, and then be radically honest. Where in your life do you need to create structure? What might that structure look like? Then do it! Put it on your "to do" list and make an appointment with yourself to get it done.**

The extent to which you live in that structure is the extent to which you'll be able to say, "I feel good about being me!"…and that's a promise!

The Futility of "Why?"

Early one morning as I was scrolling through Facebook, I came across a post that said something to the effect that the problem with the saying "Everything happens for a reason," is figuring out the reason! I guess there is some comfort in thinking that everything does happen for a reason, but many of us have had painful experiences, and have never figured out the reason.

I was reminded of this when I visited a good friend the same afternoon. Recently, she had a six- inch malignant tumor removed from her abdomen. She is one of the most spiritually minded people I know and, when first diagnosed, found herself asking the "Why?" question. You see, several years ago her husband received a similar diagnosis, and now her!

She is an RN and believes in the mind-body connection and wanted to know what more there might be that she needed to learn, because she wanted to learn the lesson and change her experience from "cancerous" to "healthful."

After investing time and energy with this process, all she could come up with was, "S*#t Happens!" That wasn't very satisfying, nor did it address the underlying spiritual issue.

As we continued our conversation, we acknowledged that, getting an answer to the "Why?" question can be helpful, and sometimes that answer seems very elusive. In the meantime, a more productive question is "What is the lesson?" What is there to learn in this situation? When we have painful and unpleasant experiences, looking for what we can learn can be powerful and transformative and we don't have to wait for the answer to appear; we can begin playing with possibilities now.

We have an Inner Magnificence and it wants only good for us. It is like an internal GPS that is programed for a life of JOY. Every experience we have contains a lesson and the lessons come in two categories: either the lesson is about some change we need to make in our thinking, or a change we need to make in behavior that will move us in the direction of a more joy-filled life. The painful lessons can be a wake-up call to change our beliefs or habits, to add new ones or get rid of old ones.

In my counseling practice, I tell my clients that we can spend our time and energy trying to figure out WHY they are the way they are, which can make for an interesting story, or we can put the same effort into developing a plan to move forward in the process of creating a life that is ultimately more joyful and satisfying. I call this the difference between interesting and important. What is always important is our next step, our next thought, our next decision.

As we go through painful experiences, instead of asking, "Why?" which can easily turn into a victim mentality, as in "Why me?" we can ask "What's the lesson, what can I learn?" These are questions that contain helpful and constructive answers.

So, here's my invitation: As you go through your day, pay attention to the lessons; pay attention to your Inner Magnificence. **When something brings you joy, find ways of doing more of it. When something stirs up pain, look for the lesson and play with ideas about what you could change that would move you more in the direction of a joyful life.**

The extent to which you do this is the extent to which you'll be able to say, "I feel good about being me!"…and that's a promise!

Get Moving!

One morning I did NOT want to get going! I had committed myself to attending a boot camp exercise class, since there was only one more opportunity before my final Spartan Race of the season. I didn't sleep well. I didn't feel rested. I just didn't feel like going! I began creating reasons why it was okay for me not to go: I've been a little banged up lately, I still have a swollen shin from the Rugged Maniac, I still have a more swollen and bruised other shin and heel from the Tuff Scrambler last week, I still have rotator cuff issues, not to mention that I dropped a heavy iron rod on my foot yesterday cleaning out the shed. I thought of lots of reasons!

I sat for forty-five minutes with my coffee cup in my hand, thinking about how nice it would be to just go back to bed! Finally, twenty-eight minutes before it was time for Boot Camp to start, I texted Heather (our trainer) and told her that I overslept and wouldn't make it this morning. I didn't really oversleep. I was just still very sleepy!

She quickly texted back: "BARY!!!" I looked at that for a second, realizing that *if I really wanted to,* I still had time to get dressed and get there. So, I did! I jumped up, got dressed, and on my way out the door, texted: "Guilt wins! I'm on my way!"

I got there just in time. It was a tough workout! But I was glad I went.

The truth is that there are lots of times that I don't want to go exercise, and I go through the same mental conversation about how I'll do it later in the day, or I tell myself I'll go tomorrow. I create lots of reasons not to go, one rationalization after another.

My wife is a morning person (no one *ever* accused me of that), and I do the same with her sometimes. She's up and ready to go to the gym and I'm still moving at my morning snail's pace. I finally tell her to go ahead, because I'm not willing to speed up and neither do I want to be an impediment to her motivation to go to the gym.

Here's the thing: I've never pushed myself to go work out and regretted that decision. On the other hand, there have been countless times when I've given in, not gone, and regretted it later.

We have an Inner Magnificence that knows what is good for us and sometimes that is enough to motivate us, but there are other times when, instead of following through, we rationalize and make excuses.

So, here's my invitation: **Follow through with your commitments to yourself, even when you don't feel like it. Consider yourself blessed if you have someone who will hold you accountable for your decisions.**

The extent to which you accept my invitation is the extent to which you'll be able to say, "I feel good about being me!"…and that's a promise!

It's Going to Be Fine

Recently we were traveling to visit family in Virginia and, on a whim, decided to see if we could visit some friends who had retired to Hickory, NC. Their roots and their remaining family are in Rhode Island, so this was a big move for them. They had to create an entirely new life for themselves, in a place where they knew nobody.

I asked my friend how they were faring, given that my wife and I have talked about doing something similar. She replied that it was fine because they decided it was going to be! They didn't talk at all about how difficult or challenging it was because they decided ahead of time that it was going to be fine!

What a powerful testimony to the philosophy that says, "Choose your thinking, create your life!"

Our life isn't really about the external condition. It is about how we choose to think about our situation and how we choose to react.

I'm sure that they did have their challenges in making such a drastic move, but because they decided it was going to be fine, they made it fine.

There is a lesson in this for those of us who might be facing challenging or difficult situations: *decide* that it is going to be fine. Then act, knowing that however it turns out will be fine. It is more than knowing; it is believing and connecting with the feeling of fine. It isn't repeating empty words. Deciding and acting are the key ingredients.

If I want my life to be fine, then a question I've found helpful is: What can I do today that will make my life five percent better? Five percent isn't a substantial number; it is less than sales tax in my state, but like compound interest, five percent over time can turn into a significant difference in our lives. Taking small steps towards our goal will create substantial changes.

When facing challenges, we have options: we can talk about how difficult the challenge is or we can paralyze ourselves into inaction, thinking about the magnitude of it all. We can decide to act, to do *something*, trusting that in one way or another our action will help us move our lives in a positive direction. Even if what we do doesn't work out the way we thought, doing something gives us information about what a more effective action might be to reach our destination.

We have an Inner Magnificence that wants us to enjoy life, that is always ready to help us move in the direction of joy. All we need to do is tune in and trust the inner guidance.

So, here's my invitation for you: **Whatever you might be facing now, decide that it is going to be fine. Hold to that belief, despite the perceived magnitude of your challenge, then act.**

The extent to which you do is the extent to which you'll be able to say, "I feel good about being me!"…and that's a promise!

Let the Dead Bury the Dead

Several years ago, I went through a dark time in my life. I felt hurt, confused, and betrayed. I was lied to and lied about. I felt victimized and ostracized. It affected me physically, coloring my personal life as well as my professional one. I was full of all kinds of emotions and none of them felt good.

This precipitated some major changes in my life, most of which have turned out to be very positive, but the process was painful!

Recently, I've encountered several people from that chapter in my life and there was a part of me that desperately wanted to be sure they knew *my side* of the story.

As I contemplated doing that, the Bible story came to mind about the man who wanted to follow Jesus but wanted to wait until he could bury his father, and Jesus responded, "Let the dead bury the dead."

This served as a reminder that what was in the past was just that: *in the past*! There is nothing I can do to change what happened. By bringing it up, I would be bringing the past into the present, and for what?

I was faced with a fundamental question: Do I want to live in the past that I can't change, or the present, which is full of potential? When I put it that way, the answer is, as they say, a "no brainer!"

How about you? Are there incidents, episodes, or chapters in your past where you felt victimized, where you felt wrongly treated or betrayed? Do you still have a desire to "set the record straight?" Do you sometimes feel the desire to share with anyone who will listen to *your side* of the story?

There comes a time when it is in our best interest to let our past R.I.P. There comes a time for us to glean whatever lessons might be found in an emotional autopsy, digging through the carnage, and then moving forward, claiming what life has in store.

There is another biblical story about Lot's wife who, as her family was escaping the destruction of what used to be their home, turned into a pillar of salt. She couldn't take her eyes off what she was losing and literally became frozen in time, unable to move forward. There's a lesson here.

No matter what our past, there is a time to move into our Magnificence, and we can't do that by continually looking backwards, by bringing up the wounds and hurts of the past, somehow hoping to change the story.

So, for any of you who also have painful chapters in your past, here's my invitation: **Let them rest in peace. Leave them in the "Cemetery of Hurts and Betrayals." Give them the final resting place they deserve and walk away, looking forward to the potential life has in store. Look around and be thankful for what is instead of continuing to mourn what once was or what might have been. There is a time to simply let it go, and that time is now!**

The extent to which you do is the extent to which you'll be able to say, "I feel good about being me!"...and that's a promise!

Monkey Theory of Management

Several years ago, when my mother was still alive, I lost weight and got myself into pretty good shape by going to the YMCA several times a week. My mother said that she wished she could do that; she knew it would be good for her, but she couldn't afford a membership. So, I bought her a three-month membership to her local Y.

A week or so later, I asked her how she liked it. She began telling me how self-conscious she felt, not knowing anybody and being in a co-ed atmosphere. I understood that, and so I bought her a membership at an all-women's gym near her home, a women-only workout facility. Problem solved!

When I checked in with her about that, she told me that she had gone, but hadn't stayed because she felt overwhelmed by all the equipment. She didn't know what to do (nor did she ask anybody for help). So, I contacted a college student, working on her master's degree in physical fitness. I connected her with my mother. The student agreed to meet my mother at the facility and help her develop a routine. and I agreed to pay for the first four sessions.

After the first session, my mother admitted that she loved her new coach, but that it was going to be too hard for them to match up schedules. I was a little astounded, given that my mother was retired and could make her own schedule every day!

By this time, I was also going to Weight Watchers and eventually meeting my goal weight and becoming a "Lifetime Member." My mother commented that she wished she could lose weight like I did but couldn't afford the program. So, I paid for a three-month membership for her. (Do you see a pattern here?) When I talked with my mother after the first meeting, she began telling me all the reasons why the Weight Watchers' program wasn't going to work for her.

Admittedly, I'm a slow learner sometimes, but I realized that my mother was more committed to talking about losing weight than she was committed to doing anything to lose weight.

It was at that point that I remembered a lesson from the first management course I ever took. It's called "The Monkey Theory of Management." In summary it teaches that when someone comes to you with a monkey on their back, when they leave, be sure the monkey is still on their back! This means that when someone comes to you with a problem, be sure that the problem still belongs to the other person when they leave. My mother kept coming to me with a monkey on her back, the problem of losing weight and getting physically healthier. My mistake was to put her monkey on my back by taking responsibility for creating her solutions.

The reality was that, in her own way, my mother preferred talking about the problem more than she preferred doing anything about it. I realized that I was getting resentful trying to solve her problem. It would have been much healthier, and loving, if I had allowed her to have her problem and simply supported her efforts at creating solutions instead of my taking responsibility for a problem that deep down, she wasn't really committed to solving.

What about you? Are you like me, a "fixer," who sometimes spends time, energy, and money trying to fix problems that rightfully belong to other people?

If so, here's my invitation: **When someone, anyone, comes to you with a problem, listen compassionately, and then assure them that they can figure out a solution. Trust their Inner Magnificence and spare yourself the experiences of burnout and resentment.**

The extent to which you accept my invitation is the extent to which you'll be able to say, "I feel good about being me!"…and that's a promise!

Newfound Freedom

Afunny thing happened on my way home from the gym. I went for a cardio kickboxing class. I got there, talked with a few friends, and looked at the board. That's when I saw that it was set up for a night of fitness testing.

That's also when I decided I wasn't going to do it: the test or the class. I stated as much to a couple of folks and started to leave. I got some pushback. "You're not going to leave, are you?" Yes, I was going to leave.

"If we have to do this, you do too!" "No, I don't!" I replied as I walked out.

This wasn't what I had come to do. I just wanted to work up a good sweat, do some cardio, some strength training, and have some fun with friends. I didn't come to do a fitness test.

Driving home, I wasn't a mile from the gym when my cell phone rang. As soon as I heard it, I knew it was my trainer. *Do I answer it…or not?* That was the question. I did answer, and it was Heather, my trainer. "Bary, that was not the workout for the kickboxing class. That was for the Fitness Adventure class later. Get your a** back here!"

There was a bit of traffic, and it took me a few minutes to turn around and get back to class. When I walked in, class had already started, and everyone had a good laugh at my expense, and I had a good workout!

There were two enjoyable experiences for me. The first was that I realized that I'm in a place in life where, when something doesn't feel like fun, I don't have to do it. I'm not making decisions based on what other people might think or expect. This is a newfound freedom for me!

The other is that I'm a part of a wonderful group of people who care about me. They cared enough to call and give me a second chance to have the workout I was looking for, to have fun!

What about you? Have you gotten to that place in life where you are free enough to do what you want and to not do what you really don't want? Are you making decisions based on what will make you happy, or are you stuck in doing what other people expect? Are you protecting some image, or are you free to be you?

We each have an Inner Magnificence and I'm here to say that there is great freedom when we make decisions that are based on what we need and want, rather than being controlled by what others might think or expect, fearing being laughed at or judged.

So, here's my invitation: **The next time you are faced with a choice between doing what is in alignment with your desires, or doing what other's might expect of you, be true to yourself. Don't think about whether others might laugh or kid or judge you for being true to yourself. After all, it's your life!**

The extent to which you honor your deeper self is the extent to which you'll be able to say, "I feel good about being me!"…and that's a promise!

Room for One More

I was scrolling through Facebook this morning and saw that my friend had posted a picture of an inviting spring table, with places for five. This was part of an event she is planning called "Friend Raising," and she invited anyone who was interested to be in touch with her if they'd like to be included.

Coupled with that was an article, I read an issue of *Psychology Today* with a cover story about loneliness. It turns out loneliness is twice as deadly as obesity.

We are hardwired for human connection, and when we feel a disconnect, it takes a toll on us. At one extreme is the adolescent who feels ostracized and acts out in angry and violent ways against his or her peers. At the other end of the spectrum are those elderly members of society, living alone, unable to drive, and feeling isolated.

Science has shown that our happiness is in direct proportion to the number of social contacts we had the day before.

I remember taking a summer job as a youth pastor in North Charleston, SC. I arrived on Saturday night and was warmly welcomed by everyone at church the next day. What I remember even more was the incredibly empty feeling I had as I watched everyone leave and go home for Sunday dinner. I had no home; I had a room on the second floor of a neighboring house. Not only was I several hundred miles from any family, I didn't even know anybody. In my aloneness, I felt very sorry for myself that day.

Fortunately, it didn't take too long for me to begin to make connections and I ended up having a wonderful summer. But I remember that empty loneliness.

We have a primal need for connections and the consequence of those feelings of loneliness can literally kill us.

So, what to do?

You can start by doing something as simple as talking to the clerk at the supermarket. Ask about their day, or what time they get to go home. That almost always makes them smile. When you are being served at a restaurant, you can learn the name of the person taking care of you; treat them like a friend instead of a servant. Or, you can be like my friend: set a table and issue an open invitation to anyone who is interested. If you are blessed with lots of social connections, remember, there is always room for at least one more.

If you are lonely, you can act in friendly ways. I know it can be difficult, but the dividends are rich. Start with the resolve to simply smile, even if you don't feel like it! You'll be surprised at the difference that gesture makes.

To those of you who are blessed with connections, **I'm inviting you 1) to appreciate the connections you have, and 2) to be intentional about reaching out to others and looking for ways to connect.**

Move into your Magnificence! Each day make it a point to be friendly and make a connection, even if it is superficial. The extent to which you do is the extent to which you'll be able to say, "I feel good about being me!"…and that's a promise!

The All-Seeing Eye

Many cultures, including our own, have used the symbol of an "all-seeing eye." We in the United States see it every time we look at our own currency, the one-dollar bill. Unfortunately, the conspiracy theorists have hijacked the symbol and turned it into something sinister, connecting it with some sort of demonic force.

Long before it made its way onto our currency, this symbol was and still is used to represent the all-seeing eye of God. The idea is that the enlightened eye of God is constantly looking over us. The creators of the dollar bill positioned it above thirteen levels of a pyramid, representing the original thirteen colonies.

Rather than arguing with those who have a different interpretation of the symbolism, I see the symbol from a perspective which points to a universal truth. I choose to see this all-seeing eye as an invitation to look beyond appearances and see life on a deeper level.

Historically, other cultures have used this symbol as a reminder that there is a way of seeing the world that doesn't get caught up in confusion and chaos, but instead sees life from a higher perspective. This perspective isn't divided into good and evil, but sees life and all its potential.

I no longer think of God as a being looking down on us, checking out and judging our behavior. Rather I think of the all-seeing eye as a way of reminding us that there is a lawful power at work in the universe—God, if you will—a force that works in logical and predictable ways. That power also emits light and the light never goes away; it either shines or gets hidden.

As a nation, there are consequences for our policies and how we conduct ourselves. To the extent to which we bear the torch of freedom, to the extent to which we stand for justice for ALL, to the extent to which we care for the widows and orphans, the elderly and the innocent, the All-Seeing Eye notices, and we are blessed.

The symbol is on our currency as a reminder that the way we use our financial resources, even as small as a dollar bill, is the extent to which we will grow and prosper as a nation—or not! How we spend our money reflects what we value, both as individuals and as a nation.

Those who designed our one-dollar bill thought of us as a nation under the watchful eye of God. Would that watchful eye be pleased with how we are loving our neighbor? How pleased might that eye be to see the way we are doing unto others? As a nation, are we spending our financial resources in ways that meet the basic needs of clean drinking water, of providing healthcare for those in need—think of the Good Samaritan—or are we, as scripture describes, laying up treasure where "moth and rust corrupt and thieves break in and steal?"

My invitation today is **to look thoughtfully at our one-dollar bill. Look especially at the All-Seeing Eye. Then do these things: 1) choose to spend that dollar in ways that meet your necessities and then find ways to spend it that feed and nourish your soul, 2) share your financial resources with those who are in need, and 3) spend your dollars in ways that reflect the Magnificence of your character. The second request is to hold our elected officials accountable for the way we spend money as a nation, in order that the Magnificence of our nation might shine over the world.**

Dr. Bary Fleet

The extent to which you do is the extent to which you will be able to say, "I feel good about being me!"…and that's a promise!

The Blame Game

I was talking with a friend last night and learned that, after twenty years on the job, she was being let go. Her local company had been bought out by a multinational corporation and they eliminated her job, just like that! They acknowledged what a valuable employee she had been, but business is business. She had worked with this company since she was nineteen; she was the glue that held everything together. Because of the strategy of mergers and acquisitions, she became a financial liability instead of a corporate asset.

Her reaction to all of this was admirable. She sees this as an opportunity, acknowledging that she probably would have stayed in the same job, doing the same thing for the rest of her career. She knows that she's going to come through this and be in a good place.

Many of us don't respond that well when we experience life-changing events, especially ones that are initiated by the principalities and powers that be. It is easy to feel victimized and blame the greedy corporate executives or whomever!

Successful people act as if they are one hundred percent responsible for their lives. Successful people don't blame or complain; they take responsibility and they act. Note that an action can be a behavior, a way of thinking and the creation of an imaginary picture of the future.

I can think of several instances in my past when I felt victimized, when I felt betrayed by those I trusted. I felt that I was treated unfairly, and that I was used as a pawn in someone else's agenda. What I know is that if I stayed in that place of playing the part of the victim, my life wouldn't get better, and I would simply become more bitter.

How about you? Are there aspects of your life where you are feeling powerless? Are you stuck blaming and complaining and acting like a victim? If so, I'm here to tell you that there are much more productive ways of responding. And the good news is that you have a choice! We always get to choose how we will respond, even when we don't choose to be in the position in which we find ourselves. Even if we know that we created an unpleasant situation for ourselves, we still get to choose our next step.

We have an Inner Magnificence that will cooperate in creating the life that we want if we are willing to step up to the plate and take responsibility for our next step. The key is claiming the power that we have, instead of looking at the powers and circumstances that are beyond our control.

So, here's the invitation: **The next time you are aware that you are feeling victimized, consciously choose how you will respond. There are no "right" or "wrong" choices; there are just choices that will get you closer to where you want to be or farther away.**

The extent to which you claim the power of how you think, the power of what you do, the power of the images you create about the future is the extent to which you'll be able to say, "I feel good about being me!"…and that's a promise.

The Company You Keep

In thinking back over the past three years at *Fitness Adventure*, a cardio kickboxing gym in my hometown, I realized that this is a community of encouragers. The members of the gym are all at various levels of fitness and everyone is striving to be their best self. As folks look at the next challenge, everyone is always encouraged to try. I've never heard a discouraging word about anyone, including myself, which is amazing, given that I am by far the oldest person there.

It's wonderful as I think about it. Whether it is the rope climb or the monkey bars, the rings or the rig, the cargo net or the sled drag, everyone is encouraged to try—when they are ready. It is an atmosphere of encouragement, not pressure.

I remember when I first approached the owner of the gym and asked if she thought I could possibly do something like a Spartan Race. Here I was, this sixty-nine-year-old guy, thinking about something way beyond my present level of conditioning.

"Absolutely!"

Her answer terrified me, as well as inspired me.

How blessed I am to have a community of encouragers!

How about you?

What kinds of people do you surround yourself with, or what kinds of people surround you? Are they the complainers and the blamers, or are they the supporters? Are they the people that stand on the sidelines and cheer for your attempts, even when it feels like failure to you, or are they the "'nay-sayers?" Are they people who share what they've learned because they want the best for you, or are they the ones who don't want to waste their time on you?

Every successful person I know has a support group of some sort. It may start with family, your spouse or parent; it may be a bunch of folks at work. It may even be something that you have to pay for, like enrolling in a class or hiring a coach, but it is a necessary ingredient in success.

We each have an Inner Magnificence and often in order to realize that, to live from it, we need encouragers in our lives; we need people who choose to see the potential in us, rather than the limitations and shortcomings. We need people who support us and build us up and want the best for us, people who accept us where we are and invite us to become more.

My invitation is two-fold: **1) Intentionally choose to be an encourager to those around you. Look for their potential, not their limitations; cheer them on toward whatever goal they might set for themselves. 2) Just as intentionally, choose to surround yourself with a group of encouragers, folks who will challenge and support you in achieving your potential.**

The extent that you do is the extent to which you will be able to say, "I feel good about being me!"...and that's a promise!

There Is No Worst Thing!

School starts the second week in August for some of my grandchildren in Virginia. I know it seems awfully early for us here in Rhode Island, but 180 days is 180 days, and they will be out by mid-May.

There were many significant changes for them, and I called to see how their first day went. As I talked to my granddaughter, she was telling me about her day and how one of the first things they did was have a "scavenger hunt" for other classmates. One of the assignments was to find two people who had two brothers. Gwen told me that she got confused, and after she found one person with two brothers, she checked that box and went on to other assignments, not realizing that the assignment was to find two people with two brothers.

I used a standard reply of mine: "If that's the worst thing that happened to you, it's been a good day!" She countered, "That wasn't the worst thing!"

Curious, I asked what the worst thing was, and—without missing a beat—she replied, "There was no worst thing! It was all good!"

I had two immediate thoughts: What an amazing experience to go through a day and not have a "worst thing!" I admired her ability to truly experience the day as being "all good!"

How many of us have something happen to us, or we do something that might be embarrassing or humiliating, and still report "It's all good!"

Sure, we say that often enough. "It's all good!" but is that how we are really feeling? It may be my projection, but I suspect that often this is a hollow phrase we tell ourselves to help soothe the disappointment.

Certainly, responding with that phrase is a step in the right direction. It is certainly better than dwelling on what seemed not to be good. Some of you are familiar with the children's book *Alexander and the Terrible, Horrible, No Good, Very Bad Day*. Some of us are Alexanders. We can list and catalogue all the experiences that aren't good; we can name all the "worst things" that happened to us.

As a second grader, I would have been horrified if I had made a mistake on a class assignment and that was brought to the attention of the entire class. (I still have a memory from second grade of being called out by the teacher!) But not Gwen! She wrote it off as simply being confused about the assignment and it was a tiny part of a day that was "all good!"

Sometimes it takes a child to help us put life in perspective. Sometimes it takes a child to help us not take ourselves too seriously.

You have an Inner Magnificence which has the ability to allow us to see all days as being good.

So, here's the two-fold challenge for today:

1) **Let's put our days in perspective and be committed to feeling positive, to seeing the goodness, no matter what.**

2) **When we so quickly say, "It's all good!" do a gut check. Is that how we feel deep inside? Is that what our heart is telling us? If so, good for us! If it is simply a phrase we use, see #1.**

The extent to which you do is the extent to which you'll be able to say, "I feel good about being me!"…and that's a promise!

To Be or To Do

If you're like me—and most people I know—you start your day with a "to-do" list. Your list might be written, or maybe you just carry it in your head (too dangerous for me; too much gets lost). I write my list not only to help me remember my agenda, but also for the joy of crossing things off and having a sense of accomplishment.

Today I invite you to begin your day with a different kind of list: a "To Be" list. It is easy to get caught up in the demands of work, family and life in general. There seem to be so many things we need to do to make life work for us and our loved ones.

Instead of focusing on all the things that you need to do today, this week, or even this month, imagine how your life might be different if you intentionally thought about how you are going to be instead.

When you first get up, how do you want to be with your spouse or your children? If you live alone, then skip on to how do you want to be at work with your colleagues? As you anticipate the events of your day, how do you want to be in each of these circumstances? If you consistently showed up as your best self, what would that look like?

How do you want to be when life throws you a curve ball, when unexpected circumstances arise?

68

As you go through your day, checking off the items on your to-do list, how do you want to be: crabby, irritable, intense, joyful, happy, or grateful? These aren't the only options and you don't have to choose just one. This is simply an invitation to set an intention.

I've learned that when I begin the day thinking about the people I will encounter, and I make a conscious decision about how I want to be, my day goes better. I feel more in charge of myself. Rather than allowing the circumstances of my day control how I am, I make a commitment to myself about how I want to be.

We each have an Inner Magnificence; we have a "best self" that is always available. The decision is whether we choose to act from that place or give the power of our reaction to external events and circumstances.

So, here's my invitation for the day: Before you begin "doing" your day, **make a conscious decision to live from your Magnificence. Make a conscious commitment about how you are going to BE.**

Take charge of your being and allow your Magnificence control how you are through the day; choose to be your best self, no matter what you are doing.

Admittedly, sometimes it will be more challenging than others, but the extent to which you choose to be your best self is the extent to which you'll be able to say, "I feel good about being me!"…and that's a promise!

Now, on to my to-do list!

What Do I See?

It wasn't my finest moment of parenting! When my daughter, who was in second grade at the time, came home with her report card, it was all "Superiors" or "A's" except for "Handwriting." That grade jumped out at me—it was "only" a "B." Wanting the best for her, I immediately announced that going forward, she would come home from school, get a snack, and then sit at the kitchen table and practice her handwriting so her next report card would be all "A's."

Any of you who have ever seen MY handwriting would pick up on the irony of this. My handwriting is very sloppy and sometimes borders on being illegible, even to me!

To this day, years later, she still remembers that moment. Instead of giving praise for the wonderful report card she brought home, I picked out the one thing that was less than perfect and made that my focus. My reaction was much more about me than about her.

I was, and still can be, more focused on what is less than perfect than on what is good and wonderful and praiseworthy.

Every time I think of this day decades ago, I cringe at the impact this had on her. I'm sure my son could also tell stories about the same dynamic; moments when my clear message was, "if it's not perfect, it's not good enough," moments when my critical side was much more evident than my encouraging side. It was well-intended, but we all know where the road of good intentions goes.

It's not enough to have good intentions, we also must have good strategies. When it comes to relationships, if our intention is to have good ones, if our intention is to encourage good ones, we need to be conscious about our focus.

We would all be well-served to look for the good in all situations, in all people. We would be well-served if we thought first about how others will receive our comments than our just wanting to be helpful.

We each have an Inner Magnificence, and life is most fulfilling when we choose to see that magnificence in others—especially our children— instead of what we might perceive as their imperfections. It is so easy for us to get caught in the trap of pointing out the mistakes, the wrong decisions, the less-than-perfect behavior, all in the name of being well-intended parents.

Here's my invitation: **If you are a parent, look for the good in your children. Catch them doing something right; give attention to that first. If you aren't a parent, or if your parenting days are behind you, do this in all your day-to-day encounters with friends and family and coworkers...and even strangers. Look first for the good, acknowledge that before being critical or offering our version of constructive criticism.**

To the extent that you move into your Magnificence, you become a person who intentionally looks for the good, who acknowledges the good before seeing the less-than-perfect. You'll not only make others feel good about themselves, you'll be able to say, "I feel good about being me!"...and that's a promise!

What's it Worth?

I learned a painful lesson when it came time to sell my parents' home of almost fifty years.

Obviously, before we children could put it on the market, we had to empty it of all the accumulated contents—and that's where we had a rude awakening. Most of the *things* in the house had great sentimental value to us. After all, they were things we had grown up with; they were souvenirs and memorabilia of trips and adventures, they were reminders of times together. They were treasures *to us!*

The painful part was when we had an estate sale. We had a "picker" come look at the contents of the house; he told us there wasn't much there worth anything, but he offered seventy-five dollars for a kitchen table and chairs in the basement. It was the set that we grew up with. We were offended at his offer and turned him down, only to end up needing to haul it to the local furniture bank because no one who came to the sale wanted the set at all. Nobody wanted the glass hand-beaded butterfly chandelier my parents bought on their trip to Italy, the chandelier that hung over the dining room table where our family gathered whenever we were together.

My wife and I recently helped a woman get her house ready to put on the market. She had a hand-woven, one hundred percent wool, nine-by-twelve carpet for which she had paid several thousands of dollars. She also had a cat that left its scent all over the carpet, and the woman was determined to sell the carpet for *a minimum* of five hundred dollars. No one even made an offer.

Here's the painful lesson: just because something has value to us doesn't mean it has value to anybody else. I am reminded of a quote from one of my son's writing professors: "Just because it happened to you doesn't make it interesting."

Anytime we want to sell something, be it an object or a service, we are well-served to refrain from thinking about what it is worth *to us* and rather think what we would be willing to pay for the object and its condition.

The reality of life is that we each get to decide what things are worth *to us* and other people are equally free to decide what things are worth *to them*.

Part of our Inner Magnificence is our own unique set of preferences and values, our style and tastes. We step into our splendor when we realize that, while something might have given us immense pleasure and joy over time, it may have no monetary value to another person.

Here's another piece to this picture: when we live from our Inner Magnificence, we also learn to let go of what no longer serves us and do so with no expectation regarding what happens next. Certainly, there is joy when another shares our tastes and preferences, but that is one of life's extras.

So, here's my invitation for today: **When you have something that you no longer need or can use, simply let it go. Return its energy back to the universe while keeping the joy of its memory with you forever.**

To the extent you do, you'll be able to say, "I feel good about being me!"…and that's a promise!

73

Who Do You Trust?

I think it might have been our first date. My current wife and I had known each other socially for a long time, but we had lost touch. We reconnected some time later at a local gym. We talked on several occasions, and she eventually invited me over for dinner. In catching up, she told me that she had been seeing somebody and that he was pursuing her heavily. Honestly, I felt jealous.

As the evening went on, she told me that she had been invited to a wedding for a friend, someone that I also knew from my past (It's a Rhode Island thing!). She went on to tell me that the man that she had been seeing had also been invited and the bride-to-be knew that he was pursuing Debbie, so the invitation didn't include the option for Debbie to bring a friend. The more I heard, the more my insecurities came to the surface.

We talked some more, and she told me that her brother had invited her to the beach for a week with his family and had told her that she was welcome to bring a friend, and would I be interested? Of course I was interested!

I was secretly hoping that, considering everything, she would decide to decline the invitation to the wedding, but she made it clear that she was going. She sensed my discomfort and looked me in the eye and asked, "Do you trust me?" She went on to say that if I didn't trust her, we didn't have any possibility for a future.

Being a guy, I told her that I trusted her, but I didn't trust HIM. My imagination was playing out all sorts of scenarios! I know what sometimes happens at wedding receptions; there is lots of alcohol, lots of dancing. Romance is in the air and stuff happens! (My therapist might suggest that I was using Freud's defense mechanism of Projection!)

She reminded me that HE wasn't the issue. The issue was whether I could trust HER!

In truth, I have no control over anybody except myself, and I don't always do a good job even with that!

There are a couple of lessons here: The first is a reminder that for any relationship to be healthy, it must be based on the people involved trusting each other. When trust is gone, there isn't much left.

The second is a reminder about control, about how, in our insecurities, we try to control other people, which never works in the long run. It is a reminder that the one person we can control is us!

We have an Inner Magnificence that shines when we decide to control what is ours to control and we release everything else.

One of the keys to life is learning to trust ourselves and choosing to trust those around us who are trustworthy.

So, here's my invitation for today: **Avoid being intimate with anyone who cannot be trusted and be trustworthy in all you say and do!**

The extent to which you accept this invitation is the extent to which you'll be able to say, "I feel good about being me!"…and that's a promise!

P.S. **As soon as you realize that you have broken a trust, own it and ask for forgiveness.** That, too, builds trust and will also allow you to say, "I feel good about being me!"

Your Comfort Zone

I f you follow me on Facebook, you know that my wife and I completed a "Rugged Maniac" event. It is a 5K mud run with twenty-five or so obstacles. Sure, we got a little banged up with bumps and bruises, but it was fun! The obstacles were designed to test our stamina, our strength, our balance, and our courage.

Some of the obstacles were beyond my physical ability, and those I simply walked around. Facing other obstacles, I took a deep breath and plunged ahead. Some of those I failed; some I surprised myself and completed, and yet others I negotiated with a little help from my friends. The fun was in facing the challenges and in the comradery.

As fate would have it, on the next day, I attended a leadership development seminar during which the facilitator talked about obstacles. She said that with every goal we have, there are action steps and there are obstacles. But here's the thing: she said that obstacles are good to have in life because they keep us from being bored. She then talked about the three zones of life: there is the Comfort Zone, where most of us live; then there is the Challenge Zone, where we try things outside of our Comfort Zone; and beyond that is the Zone of Being Overwhelmed.

She said the secret of life is to live balancing action and obstacles. If there are no obstacles, we are bored; if there is no action, we are stuck. How many of us are in that place of feeling both stuck and bored, or maybe we feel overwhelmed because the obstacles seem too big?

When we meet life's challenges head-on, our Comfort Zone expands and our lives get bigger, fuller, richer. We feel more alive.

When we begin to feel overwhelmed, we often stop stretching ourselves. When we choose to stay within our Comfort Zone, life closes in on us. We become numb and limited; we get bored and our lives wither.

The first time I finished a Spartan Beast, it took me over ten hours, sixteen plus miles, with five thousand feet of vertical climb and thirty plus obstacles, all over very rugged terrain, and I did it! I DID IT! After jumping the fire at the finish line, I went off by myself and cried. I was overwhelmed, not by obstacles that were too big, but by the feelings of having conquered obstacles bigger than I ever imagined possible for myself.

Here's the invitation for today: **Move into your Magnificence and start seeing obstacles as good things. Choose to look at obstacles as opportunities to expand your life. Look at them as opportunities to move outside of your comfort zone and feel good about yourself. Let's see them as opportunities to feel very much alive.**

And if you feel overwhelmed by life's obstacles, don't be shy about finding a coach, trainer, a cheerleader, or mentor. You'll tap into resources you never knew you had; you'll tap into your own Inner Magnificence,

The extent to which you accept my invitation is the extent to which you'll be able to say, "I feel good about being me!!"…and that's a promise!

Self-Actualization

A Bump in the Road

We live on a small street in what appears to be a quiet neighborhood. However, residents in our town know that our street serves as part of a cut-through between two main arteries. We have an inordinate amount of traffic, despite the narrow road and seemingly out-of-the-way location.

We also live in New England, notorious for its winter weather and spring potholes!

Our road is littered with potholes and, frankly, I don't want the city to fix them. I want them left alone to discourage drivers from using our street as a cut-through, and to slow them down if they do.

A considerate neighbor has hung wheel covers on a fence near the offending potholes. The not-so-nice part of me is glad that those drivers paid a price (losing their wheel covers) for their inconsiderate actions, going way too fast on our little road.

On the other hand, I don't know if there was other damage to their vehicles, like a flat tire or having the alignment of their vehicles knocked off. The evidence suggests it was simply losing part of the cosmetic appeal of the vehicle.

The truth is that as we drive down the road of life, we also hit potholes. Some are of our own making and some are simply part of the journey.

The question isn't whether we can avoid potholes in life; the question is how we will react when we do hit them.

We can feel victimized and get angry, swearing at whoever we hold responsible for allowing the pothole to be there. We can become dramatic and decide that we'll never drive down that road again. The options are limitless. Or, we can take responsibility, acknowledging that maybe we were driving too fast for the conditions or maybe we weren't being as attentive to the road as we might have been. Maybe we can retrace our path and discover that there was a Good Samaritan who made a point of recovering what was lost and leaving it where we could easily find it.

When something goes wrong in your life, do you "awful-ize" it, or are you able to acknowledge it for what it is, a bump in the road, nothing more than that? Yes, it can be a bit demoralizing. Yes, it can be inconvenient to get the issue taken care of, but it is ONLY a bump in the road!

We each have an Inner Magnificence that invites us to put everything in perspective and to know that there is "good" in everything, no matter how it seems at the time. You can even find humor in almost any situation, if you're willing to look.

For example, I used to have a car that was losing wheel covers at an amazing rate. I'll leave it to you to decide if it was because of my driving or insufficient engineering. Even at after-market prices, it got costly to replace them. Then I had an amazing realization: I only need matching wheel covers on each side of my vehicle. I only needed to buy two, not a complete set of four. No one can see both sides of the car at the same time. If your wheel covers match on the driver's side, no one will notice that the wheel covers of the passengers' side are different. It was fun!

So, here's my invitation for today: **Move into Your Magnificence and, when you hit a bump in the road of life, do two things:**

1) take responsibility, and

2) let it be simply what it is: a bump in the road. Refuse to catastrophize it and rob you of the joy of your journey.

The extent to which you do is the extent to which you'll be able to say, "I feel good about being me!"…and that's a promise!

Conscious Conversation

Often, it isn't what you say, it's how you say it.

John Gottman has been studying couples for decades and, after spending just fifteen minutes with a couple, he can predict with better than ninety percent accuracy whether they will still be together five years down the road.

Gottman tracks four distinct aspects of communication, and the extent to which they show up is the gauge he uses to make his prediction. He calls them the Four Horsemen of the Apocalypse, and they are Criticism, Contempt, Defensiveness, and Stonewalling. When couples are talking about any topic that stirs emotion, these are the culprits that will ultimately destroy a relationship.

Let's look at them:

CRITICISM: We sometimes joke at home that, "As long as we know who to blame, that is the important part." We can joke, because we know that nothing good comes from blaming. When we are honest, the problem is never about who did what; it is always about how I am reacting to what you have, or have not, done. The remedy is to shift the conversation from making "You" statements to "I" statements, keeping the focus on how I feel instead of what You did!

CONTEMPT: Any time we are in a conversation and we talk to the other person as if they are beneath us, it destroys any desire to be close. Contempt can be expressed in words or behavior. Yes, this includes the classic eye roll. When we don't feel respected, when we are treated as less, there is no desire for connection.

DEFENSIVENESS: When we try and talk with someone and they aren't willing to own their own behavior, or we aren't willing to take responsibility for our part of a situation, where can the relationship go? There is no room for connection; we are left feeling alone.

STONEWALLING: It can be so frustrating to try and talk with someone who won't talk. They don't say a word, or they answer our question with "I'm fine!" and we know, whatever they are, they aren't fine! It is an effective conversation killer.

Whether it is a marriage or a friendship, whether it is a colleague at work or a neighbor, if the relationship isn't what you'd like it to be, check the four horsemen.

If we want a healthy relationship with someone, we are well-advised to be conscious not only of what we say, but how we say it.

Not only do we have an Inner Magnificence, so does everyone else. Just like we want to be treated respectfully, so is everyone worthy of being treated respectfully, no matter what they said or did.

So, here's my invitation for today: **Make a conscious choice to eliminate the four horsemen from your conversations, all your conversations, even the ones on Facebook.**

If you are married, you'll have a better chance of still being married five years from now. If you aren't married, you'll have better relationships with everyone in your life.

The extent to which you accept my invitation is the extent to which you'll be able to say, "I feel good about being me!"…and that's a promise!

A Different Perspective

It's not one of my more noble qualities. I know that often my first response is one of judgment!

Today at the library, I intentionally sought out the room with several "Quiet Zone" signs posted around. I was enjoying the quiet when a woman came in, sat down beside me, and took out her cell phone. First were the intrusively loud beeps as she dialed a number. Then in a loud and irritating voice, she dictated a message, a rather long message, the bottom line of which was that she missed her bus and it would be more than an hour before she could get another one.

Immediately I felt offended by her lack of regard for the space we were in, and then my frontal cortex kicked in, asking if there was another way I could perceive what was happening. It didn't take me long to think about the fact that I drove here, and I could leave whenever I wanted. I wasn't at the mercy of the bus schedule. I then looked outside and, noticing that it was raining torrents, was immensely grateful that I didn't have to stand outside in the rain at the bus stop, waiting for the next one.

As I began to be aware of how different my life circumstance is from this stranger whose cell phone use had interrupted my sanctuary of silence, my irritation melted into compassion and gratitude.

Admittedly, I don't always stop and think, I just react, but when I do make the choice to allow for the possibility of a bigger picture, I end up feeling much better.

It is so easy to criticize the behavior of another, at least for me it is, and never consider their back story. It is easy for me to forget that what I take for granted, and others lack. I'm referring to simple things, like the freedom to get in my car and go where I want when I want, and being able to decide that I'm hungry or thirsty and swing into some drive-through and have my desires met.

How about you? What about the judgments and irritations you allow to get stirred up by those random incidents and people you encounter?

I'm here to say that there is always a more compassionate way of thinking, if we're willing to open ourselves to it. There is a reason for that adage of "If you want to understand someone, walk a mile in their shoes."

We all have an Inner Magnificence, even those people who ride the bus and who ignore the "Quiet Zone" signs at the library!

Here's my invitation for today: **When you find yourself feeling irritated by the behavior of someone around you, move into your Magnificence. Stop and remind yourself that they have a story, and it may well be that, if you knew it, you'd respond with compassion for them, and renewed gratitude for your own blessings!**

The extent to which you do is the extent to which you'll be able to say, "I feel good about being me!"…and that's a promise!

Don't Push

A pane of glass on the front door of my gym was broken. Someone covered the hole with a piece of cardboard and then put up a sign that read: "Don't push on window!"

Words have great power to shape our behavior, and very few of us like to be told what not to do. "Don't Push!" almost becomes an invitation. There is that rebellious part in most of us that takes delight in doing something we're told not to do.

Life always responds better to a positive than a negative. What if the cardboard sign had simply read, "Be careful!"

In life, we get much better results when we think about what we want than what we don't want. The problem is that sometimes it is easier to articulate what we don't want than what we do want. If we think about looking at a compass, it is easy to say, "I don't want to go this way," but that leaves 359 other options on the compass in terms of directions. It is much more productive to say, "This is the heading I want to take!" We've just eliminated 359 other options and found the one that will get us to our destination. And if it turns out that our decision isn't quite getting us where we want to be, we can always refine and change, but at least we're moving in the general direction we want to go.

Move Into Your Magnificence

There is a part of our imagination that doesn't compute a negative; it only deals with images. Putting a "not" in front of the image leaves the image intact. It is the suggested image that conveys the power. Imagine me telling you, "No matter what, under risk of death, do not...absolutely DO NOT IMAGINE a green giraffe." What did you just do? Yes, a green giraffe flashed across the screen of our imagination!

It isn't just words that are powerful, it is images. Every sports psychologist encourages their client to imagine success before the competition, whether it be sinking the putt or scoring a clutch basket or serving an ace in tennis. That visual image helps create our experience. Instead of thinking about avoiding the rough, a golfer imagines the ball landing on the fairway, or on the green. When serving, a tennis player imagines the ball going exactly where they are aiming; they eliminate any thought of a mistake and focus on exactly what they are wanting to do.

Move into your Magnificence. For example, instead of telling (yelling at) your children to stop hitting each other, tell them that you want them to get along. Instead of telling your spouse to stop leaving his (yes HIS) dirty laundry on the floor, ask him to be mindful of putting his dirty laundry in the hamper.

If there is something that you desire, tell people what you want them to do, not what you don't want them to do. Always frame your request in terms of the desired outcome rather than the absence of an unwanted behavior. It may seem silly, but it is the wording and the images that have the power.

So, here's my invitation: **Move into your Magnificence, state clearly your wants and desires, and express them in positive images.**

The extent to which you accept my invitation is the extent to which you'll be able to say, "I feel good about being me!"...and that's a promise!

Eye to Eye

When it comes to driving, I can be as aggressive as the next person. I'm not proud of that, just stating a fact.

The other day traffic was especially heavy on I-95, and two on-ramps were merging just before the ultimate merger onto the interstate. We were in the right lane, and as we got closer to the interstate, the drivers from both the left and right merge lanes were doing "zipper" merging: each lane was alternating, and it was working well, that is until the woman to my left refused to let me have my turn at merging.

The more primitive me started to edge over and see if I could force her to back off. She was having nothing of it. She just kept inching closer and closer to the car in front of her, sending the clear message that she was not going to let me in. At first, my aggressive self got caught up in the challenge. I looked over at her, hoping to make eye contact, but she, being a seasoned player, had her eyes locked on the bumper of the car in front of her. There was no way she was going to look at me.

It was in that moment that I realized the silliness of what was happening: I was being invited to participate in a power struggle. I chose not to, backed off, and let her go ahead. I wish that was the end of the story, but once we got out on the highway, I quickly ascertained which lane was moving faster, and I jumped into that before "she" could, and

I took great delight in passing her. She won the battle, but I won the war! You can bet that I made a point of trying to make eye contact with her when I passed her, but once again she pretended to ignore me. She wasn't going to give me the satisfaction of winning.

It was at that point that I felt embarrassed over my own behavior: all of this angst over a single car length in a ten mile trip!

How easy it is for me—and I suspect many of us—to get caught in silly power struggles. How easy it is for us to allow our ego to take over and cause us not only to do silly things, but also dangerous things.

What's your "hook?" What is it that strikes at the heart of your sense of self-importance? What is it that causes you to make up a story about how disrespectfully you are being treated?

As I think back, I don't know whether I was upset because the other driver wouldn't even look at me, or if I would have been more upset had she looked me in the eye and continued to refuse to let me merge. I think being treated as if I don't even exist stirs up one set of emotions, while being openly challenged by the stare-in-your-face look stirs up another.

What I know is that when we allow our egos to rule, it rarely ends well.

So, here's my invitation: **The next time someone challenges you—or acts in a way that your ego leads you to conclude you're being challenged or disrespected—let it go. I know, this is easier said than done! What I also know are two things: 1) there was nothing personal about her refusing to allow me to merge; it wouldn't have mattered who I was, that's just the way SHE chose to act, and 2) when I make the conscious choice not to allow ego to rule, I always feel better about me.**

Life isn't about winning; it is about being our best selves.

When you make a decision based on being your best self, based on your Inner Magnificence, you'll be able to say, "I feel good about being me!"…and that's a promise!

Face the Fear

I usually take the stairs; recently I had to go up five flights and I was carrying a heavy book bag and my hands were full, so I opted for the elevator. I entered the elevator on the first floor and a woman got on right behind me. Since I was closest to the buttons, I asked which floor and she said, "Two, please." I noticed that she was carrying her coat and had her purse clutched close to her chest. I commented with a smile, "Short trip!"

She smiled and said, "I'm terrified of elevators and I'm tired of it, so, every day I make myself get in one and go at least one floor." I commended her for her willingness to face her fear, and her courage in doing something about it.

Years ago, Susan Jeffers wrote a book called, *Feel the Fear, and Do It Anyway*.

I began thinking about all the opportunities I have had and didn't take advantage of because I was afraid. Going to the top of the Eiffel Tower comes to mind—a once-in-a-lifetime opportunity and I missed it because I was afraid. Touching the snake that my grandsons are holding is another. Turning down an invitation to go have my picture taken holding the Stanley Cup with Lou Lamoriello, then coach of the New Jersey Devils is yet another. I turned down the opportunity because it was at the home of a woman I hardly knew, and I thought I'd be self-conscious and uncomfortable in the presence of a lot of other people I didn't know. If I reflected for very long, I'm sure the list of experiences that I have denied myself—little pieces of joy—just because I was afraid is *frighteningly* long.

Many of us have phobias, irrational fears. We know on some level that we are safe, and we can acknowledge that our fears are irrational, and we continue to allow them to control us, to limit us, and keep our lives small. It was refreshing to ride the elevator with someone who was tired of living that way, a courageous woman who was willing to make a conscious decision to face her fear and do it anyway!

Ralph Waldo Emerson once said, "He who is not every day conquering some fear has not learned the secret of life."

We have an Inner Magnificence that wants you to know the secret of life, that flourishes when we choose courage.

What about you, what is the elevator you need to get on?

So, here's my invitation to you: **Choose to live life bravely; enter new experiences. Consciously choose to not allow your life to be limited by your fears.**

The extent to which you accept my invitation is the extent to which you'll be able to say, "I feel good about being me!"…and that's a promise!

Financial Freedom

A mutual friend connected me with Marco, a financial advisor. We met for lunch and, during our conversation, he proclaimed that for the most part, we aren't taught how to manage money, how to save money, or how to grow money; we are taught to spend money. We are a society of consumers, not a society of savers or investors.

I know that my dad never taught me about money; this isn't a judgment, because he grew up on a farm and never learned much about money, except how to get along when you don't have much. Following in his footsteps, I never really made it a point to learn about money either, but I sure know how to spend! I know how to consume!

When it comes to buying and spending, Robert Kiyosaki in his book *Rich Dad, Poor Dad*, says that the rich buy investments, the poor buy things, and the middle class buys things that they think are investments.

Along the way, I decided to learn about money and one of my first lessons was to never borrow money to buy something that depreciates. Never charge anything you know you can't pay for when the bill comes in. That's a challenge when credit cards are so easy to come by. This, by the way, even includes automobiles! Think about what it would be like to pay cash for your car and then, instead of making payments

94

to a lender, invest the equivalent amount each month, allowing that money to be earning interest and then, when the time comes, using that money to pay cash for the next car.

John Wesley, a spiritual forbearer, taught that we should save ten percent of everything we earn, give away ten percent of everything we earn, and live on the rest. It represents a philosophy of "pay yourself first." Most of us, me included, have bought into (pun intended) the notion that our happiness is connected to our things. In doing so, many of us have created lives with the chronic stress of trying to pay our bills. A Harris Poll done in November of 2017 showed that the average American pays well over a thousand dollars a year in credit card interest alone, not including auto and home mortgage interest payments.

We have an Inner Magnificence that deserves better than to live a life of servitude, a life of indebtedness. How would you react if I said that I would give you one thousand dollars a year each year that you don't incur any interest charges on any credit card debt? Or think in terms of saving over a hundred dollars a month to put toward a vacation or some luxury that you could buy with cash.

Our Magnificence wants us to live in joy and freedom, not with burdens of debt and financial worries. To do that might mean that we need to cut back on our lifestyle a bit, but in exchange there comes a lightness about our lives.

One of the solid principles of money management is to save money and pay cash for everything except your home. Isn't that a "magnificent" way to live?

So, that's my invitation, my challenge: **Live each day only buying what we have the cash to pay for, or never have credit card debt that you can't pay off when the statement comes. Once we make the adjustment, we'll discover how incredibly freeing life can be.**

The extent to which you free yourself from debt is the extent to which you'll be able to say, "I feel good about being me!"…and that's a promise!

Follow Your Heart

She was our server at a farm-to-table restaurant in Virginia Beach. As the evening progressed, we got a chance to learn a little bit about her. It turned out that she earned a degree in Hospitality Management and got the "job of her dreams," working with a professional sports venue. The problem was: she hated it!

What do you do when you end up in a circumstance like that?

She made a very courageous move. She quit! She talked with her husband and then she called the owner of this restaurant and asked if she could come and work as part of the wait staff. He was happy to have her, and four years later she is still there as a server. She doesn't know how long she'll stay, but what she knows is that she has a job that she loves and that's what matters! She enjoys her relationship with her employers and her relationship with her customers, not to mention that she loves the concept of the restaurant and the food!

She chose passion over economics. She chose doing something she loves over doing something that pays better. She chose to pay attention to her feelings instead of being practical.

I saw a post on Facebook this morning (I didn't pay attention to who posted it) that said: "Who is happier than a teacher? Answer: A retired teacher." I get it: it isn't the job itself, but all the other stuff that the administration requires (and that is a conversation worthy of having at another time).

But the question remains: What do you do when you have a job that doesn't call to your heart?

There are ALWAYS options, but sometimes the options come at an economic price. It takes courage to swallow your pride, like she did, and say, "Yes, I have a college degree, and I'm choosing to work as a server at a restaurant I love." Sometimes it takes courage to say, "I'm going make a choice to put my inner happiness over my bank account." Sometimes it takes courage to walk away from a job that so many others think they'd love to have in exchange for a job that very few people would want.

Many people I know live from weekend to weekend…dreading the five days in between. Many are counting the years/months/days until they can retire. It's an economic decision, but the price is that they die a little inside every day. I know; I've been there.

Joseph Campbell taught, "Follow your bliss, and the money will follow." Confucius said, "Choose a job you love, and you'll never work a day in your life." What I know is that when we truly follow our bliss, when we are doing something we love, we come alive.

So, here's my invitation: Listen to your heart. Maybe right now you truly can't afford to just up and quit the job you dread going to each day, but what you can do is to move your Magnificence and connect with something that stirs your passion, something that makes you feel alive. Maybe that's the trade-off…you have "a job" to go to that allows you to do something that you love.

One way or another, **give yourself permission to live your life doing something that you love.**

The extent that you do is the extent to which you'll be able to say, "I feel good about being me!"…and that's a promise!

A Heart-Broken Face

We had put cute construction equipment name tags on gift bags for our grandsons, and I wanted to re-use them. I was carefully working at removing the first sticker when the three-year-old brought me his bag and began to remove the sticker with his name. I was aware of how tedious the process was and asked him not to do it because "you have to be very careful."

It was a painstaking process and, as I successfully finished removing the first sticker, I heard my grandson tear his. I was irritated and rebuked him by saying, "I said 'You have to be careful!'"

He looked at me with teary eyes and replied, "But I WAS being careful!"

It was only as I saw the tears that I realized that yes, he was being as careful as a three-year-old can be! But that wasn't good enough for this project!

I had an agenda, and he had ruined it by doing his best!

If I had only been listening with my heart instead of from my agenda. I mean, really, were the stickers that valuable? Only in my mind at that moment. The truth is that I could go online and get a package of twenty-four of those stickers for less than a couple of bucks.

What was truly valuable in that moment was my grandson's heart, and I broke it by telling him that doing his best wasn't good enough!

He will never remember that moment, but I will.

In and of itself, that moment isn't a big deal, but in that moment, I planted a seed that, if watered and fertilized by myself and others on future occasions, will grow and develop into an inferiority complex. It is a seed that will erode his self-esteem.

This was a painful reminder for me to listen from my heart and to listen to the heart of whomever else is with me.

Had I stopped and comforted him in his pain of having failed to remove the sticker successfully, we would have created a bond. We would have connected, and I would have planted a different kind of seed. I would have reinforced a painful life lesson that sometimes, even when we do our best, we don't get the desired results and, in those moments, we can find comfort knowing that we did our best!

I did give him a hug and tell him it was okay, but will he remember my rebuke or my hug?

Who doesn't want someone around us to comfort us in times when our best doesn't get us what we want, instead of rebuking us for not being good enough?

So, here's my invitation: **Move into your Magnificence. Forget your agenda, whatever it is, and listen with your heart; listen to the heart of others.**

The extent you do is the extent to which you'll be able to say, "I feel good about being me!"…and that's a promise!

Letter of Absolute Assurance

I was catching up on mail, having just been away for ten days. After throwing out the junk mail, I began opening the first-class mail. One of the letters was from an institution which has previously employed me. It was in the standard form of a memo: To, From, Date, Re. It was the "Re." section that caught my eye. It was a "Letter of Reasonable Assurance" regarding future employment. I've never received anything like this before.

On the one hand, it was reasonably assuring, but the memo was also very clear that things could change at any time. The letter was highlighting the fact that this is NOT a legally binding contract. The institution could change its mind at any time for any reason, or for no reason, and I would have no recourse.

I began thinking about all agencies and institutions in life about which I have reasonable assurance and those in which I have absolute assurance. I am reasonably assured that my Social Security check will come each month, but who knows what some future Congress might decide or what the future economy of our nation might look like? Along the same lines, I am reasonably assured regarding my future pension, but again, there is no absolute guarantee regarding the future of the economy.

It has been said that there are only two areas in our lives in which we have absolute assurance: death and taxes. I would add an even bigger area. Even though I don't always feel this way, I am absolutely assured that good will overcome all that we perceive as evil.

What I'd like to do is to write you a letter of complete assurance. Whether or not you think it is reasonable is up to you, but I am absolutely convinced.

So .... Memo:

TO: You
FROM: Me
DATE: Today
RE: Letter of Absolute Assurance

This letter provides absolute assurance that you have an Inner Magnificence.

I am absolutely convinced that we all have a sacred core, sort of like a stem cell of the Divine. At our core, we are made up of all that is good.

No matter how you feel, no matter what you do, or don't do, no matter what has happened to you in the past, nothing can take away from your Inner Magnificence. Sure, it can get covered up, but it never goes away. It never gets damaged and it is eternally present.

So, my invitation is for you to **move into that Magnificence and live from that place which is courageous and honorable, true and just, compassionate and loving, generous and kind, and strong and focused.**

Any time you have doubts, reread this letter of Absolute Assurance of the truth of who and what you are!

The extent to which you accept my invitation is the extent to which you'll be able to say, "I feel good about being me!"...and that's a promise!

Little Decisions

How many decisions do you think you will make today? Most of the research I found says that, by the end of the day, we will have made about thirty-five thousand. Thirty-Five Thousand little decisions!

Some time ago there was a popular book called *Don't Sweat the Small Stuff* and, while I understand what the author was saying, I'm convinced that it's the small stuff that ultimately matters.

Do I get up now, or hit the snooze button? What do I put in my coffee, if anything? What do I have for breakfast? What do I wear (lots of decisions involved here)? Do I even have breakfast? How fast do I drive to work? Do I get gas on the way home, or first thing in the morning? Do I let that other car merge, or do I squeeze it out? Do I smile?

C.S. Lewis, one of my favorite authors, said in his book *Mere Christianity*, "Good and evil both increase at compound interest. That is why the little decisions you and I make every day are of such infinite importance."

The latest research suggests that Alzheimer's begins in our brain thirty years before there are any outward symptoms. The little decisions we made every day either speed up, or slow down the process. What did we choose to drink? Did we choose sweets or vegetables, processed food or fresh? Not one of those decisions will alone make a difference, but together they chart our destiny.

Every decision we make about what to eat or drink either adds to our health, or takes away from it. Our current state of health is the result of thousands of little decisions.

The same is true for our character. We have an Inner Magnificence, and every little thing we say, every little thing we think either reveals our Magnificence...or covers it. Every time we're even a little bit dishonest, every little act toward "getting even," every little attitude of superiority, every little decision to act in a way that is less than loving covers our Magnificence. Here's the kicker: it makes it harder for us to live from our Magnificence, and it makes the world less likely to see us in our Magnificence.

Every word that comes out of our mouth—or doesn't—either contributes to the amount of kindness in the world or diminishes it, either contributes to peace or diminishes it. Every little decision we make about what we say and how we say it, every little decision about the choice of words makes a difference.

So, here's my invitation for today: **Make conscious decisions. Before you do ANYTHING, ask yourself if what you are about to do—or say—will contribute to your overall wellbeing, or diminish it. Will it help reveal your Magnificence, or cover it? Then, chose wisely!**

The extent to which you do is the extent to which you'll be able to say, "I feel good about being me!"...and that's a promise!

A Little Help from Your Friends

This past weekend a group from our gym completed an obstacle course race together. One of the differences from other races was we were not being timed. It was just an event, an experience. This allowed me to set aside my competitive nature and enjoy a group experience.

Instead of each of us trying to get our best personal time, we ended up doing the obstacles together. Clearly, some of our group could have gone much faster, but chose to stay together. Some of us did obstacles while others chose to walk around them. Several of us were able to complete various obstacles with a little help from each other. Occasionally, that meant a few of us had to wait while other members of our group completed, or attempted to complete, various obstacles, but instead of the faster ones going on ahead, we all hung together, starting and finishing together!

We even took time at the end to organize ourselves enough so we could all hold hands and cross the finish line together, a gesture of solidarity, of teamwork. We all acknowledged that it was great fun doing the event that way instead of being obsessed with our finishing time.

I think this is a wonderful metaphor for life in general. It can be a lot of fun when we set aside our competitive nature and decide to simply enjoy the experience and each other.

Yes, it is also fun to challenge ourselves and strive for our personal best in whatever we are doing, but it is also fun to just be with the people we're with and not think about time.

What about you? Are you stuck in a place of comparison, wanting to know how you stack up against others in general, or can you simply enjoy being with the group?

By definition, there can only be one first place, but there can be an almost infinite number who can enjoy doing things together.

As I look around, I see a lot of people who are making decisions based on what is good for them, and not thinking about the rest. Yes, there is a level of pleasure that comes from bettering our position, but as someone once said, "It is lonely at the top."

When I think about myself, I like the joy of being surrounded by friends and colleagues who are sharing my life, my experience, my struggles, and my triumphs, and I love being around those who allow me to share theirs.

We each have an Inner Magnificence and it is programed to help us feel good about being who we are. In my research on what allows people to feel good about themselves, there are two answers that show up consistently: 1) "When I do something I didn't think I could do" and 2) "When I do something that makes a difference for somebody else."

So, here's my invitation for today: **Find a way to be a part of a team that allows you to work together. It might be as simple as enlisting your children to team up with you to clean the house. A team can be as small as two, or as large as a nation! What is important is that you are working together on a common goal.**

The extent to which you decide to share an experience with others is the extent to which you'll be able to say, "I feel good about being me!"…and that's a promise!

Host or Hostage

I was listening to a podcast by Dr. Wayne Dyer one day and he closed with a powerful quote: "We can either allow ourselves to be a host to God or a hostage to Ego." In my writing, I seldom use the word "God" because it stirs up negative connotations for so many people I know. That's why the concept I offer is our "Inner Magnificence." Whatever language we use, whatever terminology we use, Dyer offers a powerful challenge.

Speaking of terminology, I would quibble a bit about Dyer's use of "Ego" because, as a psychologist, I contend he is referring to our Id. According to Freud's theory, the Id is the part of us that causes us simply to do whatever feels good in the moment. It has no concern for consequences or consideration of others.

Dyer's question is about what force we allow to control our lives, to control our decision-making. Right now, sadly, it seems we have government officials, from the president on down to most of Congress, and extending on down to the local levels who are hostage to self-centered forces. This is evidenced by the policies that are being made and the way these policies are being implemented. It is evidenced even through the language public figures are using in their political speeches and campaign rhetoric.

The reality is that, while we may have no control over their behavior, we are free to choose how we live our own lives; we are free to choose how we think about the circumstances in which we find ourselves, and how we treat the people with whom we interact.

When we "host" our Inner Magnificence, when we allow ourselves to connect with our highest and best self, we understand that everything and everyone in this universe is intricately connected. We realize that everything we do impacts everything and everyone around us. When I act from that Magnificence, I make the world a better place, and I contribute to the lives of people I may not even know. My Magnificence has a ripple effect for good.

When we choose to live from our Magnificence, we walk through life with our heads held high, proud of who we are, proud of how we conduct ourselves. We go through life with a sense of joy and freedom and appreciation. When we are hostage to our egos (as Dyer refers to it), when we act as if we are better than others, when we have the need to belittle others, we unwittingly miss out on the joy that is our life's treasure. As hostages to our ego, we build self-imposed prisons. We deny ourselves the freedom to enjoy ourselves no matter where we go or with whom we find ourselves. We build walls around ourselves.

So, here's my invitation for today: **Live from your Magnificence; be a host for God, for all that is Good. Let your energy be light and love for all.**

The extent to which you do is the extent to which you'll be able to say, "I feel good about being me!"…and that's a promise!

Love Story

We are looking forward a trip to South Carolina to join in the wedding celebration of my youngest niece. There have been lots of pictures chronicling their love story, lots of posts on Facebook brimming with excitement and joy. I remember those feelings!

We have an Inner Magnificence that desires relationship, that flourishes in intimacy. Sometimes we get caught up in the romantic expression of love and forget that love is so much more, so much richer than romance. We get so caught up in the happiness we feel when in the presence of our beloved, in the joy we get in bringing happiness to our beloved, and we lose sight of the other experiences that are bound to come.

I don't know anybody who has fallen in love with a person who hasn't also been hurt by that person. I don't know anybody who has fallen in love and not done or said hurtful things to their beloved. These occurrences don't even have to be intentional; they come from simply living under the same roof. The very act of becoming vulnerable with someone sets us up for the possibility of experiencing hurt.

As spring comes and the wedding season begins, this is an appropriate time to reflect on the multifaceted aspects of love.

My experience suggests that there are at least four strands of love when it comes from our Inner Magnificence. The first is the ability to love ourselves. To set ourselves up for success in any relationship, we must first learn to love the person we see in the mirror.

Only then can we take the second step of truly loving another, offering our whole heart. Only then can we be fully present with them in their experiences with life, the ups and downs, the good and the bad, their successes and their seeming failures.

The third facet has to do with being able to truly celebrate the good that happens in the life of our partner. Sometimes when our partner brings home a story of success, our first thought has to do with how this is going to affect us. Our reactions become about us instead of for the one we love.

Finally, I think love is about balancing our needs and wants with those of our partner. One of the conflict resolution techniques I teach is to have the aggrieved partner start by saying, "What I want FOR you is...." The problem is that our complaint is often limited to communicating what we want FROM our partner. It gets tricky, this thing of balancing our needs and wants with the needs and wants of the other, tricky but vital!

Falling in love is easy, but being consistently loving isn't, at least in my experience. The core of our Inner Magnificence is love, a never-ending invitation to experience it and express it.

So, here's my invitation: **The next time you feel hurt, the next time you feel insecure in your relationship, stop and reflect on the loving response. Think about the response that honors both yourself and the other, and then do it!**

The extent to which you do is the extent to which you'll be able to say, "I feel good about being me!"...and that's a promise!

Memories

I watched a grandmother taking her grandson out on the front porch. She sat down and held him in her lap as they faced the ocean, and she began talking to him about what they were seeing. I guessed the boy was about ten months old. What I knew was that he would never remember that morning, never remember that time of being held in her lap, never remember what she told him about the view. But what I also knew was that somewhere deep in his soul, he would have good feelings about his grandmother and a longing for the ocean. He just wouldn't remember that this particular morning was a part of creating those feelings.

In a much earlier chapter of my life, I was partially responsible for the Sunday school curriculum for twelve hundred or so local churches. It was my job to help them choose an appropriate curriculum, while sharing feedback with the publishing house about the issues faced by the consumer. I also led training sessions for the volunteer teachers regarding their curriculum options.

Many of the volunteers felt very inadequate as teachers. One of the truths I shared with them is that their students would absorb the information and Bible stories, but not attribute any of it to a particular teacher. What the students would remember was how the teacher made them feel. They would remember teachers who made them feel loved, and they would remember teachers who criticized and chastised them. They would remember teachers who encouraged them, and they would remember teachers who demeaned them. It's the feelings that leave a mark, not the information. It's the messages they got about themselves that they would remember and attribute to a specific teacher.

Think about your elementary school teachers. What do you remember about them? I bet you remember whether you had a good experience with them, or a not-so-good experience. If you remember anything, you remember the feelings associated with being in their class.

My first grade teacher was very structured and taught me to work independently; my second grade teacher resented having me in her class (that's another story, and it had nothing to do with me personally); my third grade teacher was pretty and I fell in love with her; my fourth grade teacher I don't remember at all; my fifth grade teacher was okay; my sixth grade teacher made me feel welcome and I was happy to have her again in the seventh grade.

What people remember about us is not all the details of what we did or didn't do; what they will remember is how they made us feel about ourselves.

Here's the invitation for today: **Make a conscious choice to relate to people—family, friends, and strangers—in a way that will make them smile, in a way that will make them feel good about themselves.**

You have an Inner Magnificence and so does EVERYBODY. Make the choice to be up-lifting and encouraging, to be affirming and caring. Don't think about whether your words and actions will be remembered, just relate with kindness!

The extent to which you accept my invitation is the extent to which you'll be able to say, "I feel good about being me!"…and that's a promise!

Mother's Day

It was Mother's Day and while I was talking to a friend, she confided that Mother's Day is a very difficult day for her. "She was a real bitch!" was how she described her mother. "How am I supposed to feel?" Later, I asked another woman what she was doing for the day and she replied, "Well, I'm not a mother, so I guess I'll go home and be with my cats." There was a sadness in her voice and her face. These conversations got me to thinking about Mother's Day and how difficult it can be for many people.

Many of us were blessed with mothers who were loving and nurturing, not perfect, but who "mothered" us to the best of their abilities. It is appropriate that we stop and give honor to those women and that gift.

There are a multitude of others for whom this day is very tough. Some of us were not "mothered," but were abused—physically and/or emotionally. Some of us grew up mothering our mothers because they couldn't take care of themselves emotionally, let alone others. Some of us grew up without a mother, due to a tragic loss. Some of us were given birth to by women who not only didn't seem to have a clue about how to be a mother, but also resented the obligation of being one. Some of us grew up with mothers who were more absent than present, both emotionally and physically.

Then, there are those whose life's dream was to become a mother and never had that. experience. For them, Mother's Day is a reminder of what they never could be, leaving them with a hollow longing. Some women *were* mothers, but lost their child from disease or other tragedy. For them, Mother's Day is profoundly sad and empty.

Some of us were given up for adoption by women who knew they were not able to be a mother and, on this day of all days, are reminded of a painful chapter from their past. Others were adopted, and don't know the story of their birth mother; many in that group wonder why the woman who gave birth to them didn't value them enough to keep them.

There are school children who see their classmates making Mother's Day cards to take home, and they are reminded that they don't have a mother at home to celebrate.

My point is that, in the midst of honoring the role and contribution of mothers, it is important to be mindful and sensitive to those for whom this is a difficult day.

Mother's Day is a time to honor the mothering we have received, and to claim all the nurturing we have been given. It is a time not only to celebrate the idea of the biological mother, but the maternal energy we have received. Some of us have received this from our birth mother and we miss her presence dearly; some of us continue to receive this from her, and value it deeply. Some are grateful that there were other women—and sometimes men—who nurtured and cared for us the way a mother might.

So, on Mother's Day, my invitation is to move into your Magnificence and celebrate all the people who have contributed to making you the person you are and commit to be a "mothering" presence in the lives of all we meet who are hurt, lonely, or afraid.

The extent to which you do is the extent to which you'll be able to say, "I feel good about being me!"…and that's a promise!

Radical Acceptance

"God, grant me the serenity to accept the things I cannot change; courage to change the things I can; and the wisdom to know the difference."

While there remains controversy about who originally wrote it, the Serenity Prayer has been a staple in the Alcoholics Anonymous program for decades. It's very simple in its language, but—like many teachings—easier said than done.

Marsha Linehan pioneered a type of therapy known as Dialectical Behavior Therapy, and one of the cornerstones is what she calls "Radical Acceptance."

The underlying truth is that there are aspects of life that we need to simply accept as being what they are, period. Many of us make ourselves miserable in our belief that certain situations and conditions *should be* different.

This can apply to the circumstances in which we find ourselves. It can apply to the people in our lives. It can also apply to our perception of ourselves. We can all be judgmental in our expectations about life, about others, and about ourselves.

The reality is that those judgments do not allow us to live happier lives. Those judgments are often the source of great frustration and even anger, and those judgments are self-created!

What would it be like if we got rid of our notions of how things *should be* and accepted how they *are?* This radical acceptance of life becomes the beginning point for happiness, for joy.

"How?" you may ask. That's where the Serenity Prayer comes into play. Once we accept how things are, we begin a discernment process and sort things into two piles.

The first pile contains all the experiences we cannot change. No matter how much we'd like to change various aspects of life and some of the people in our lives, the power to effect change is simply not ours. There is a certain peacefulness that follows when we acknowledge our limitations in terms of changing situations and people.

The second pile contains the situations and circumstances that we can change, if we have the courage to tackle them. We can change our reactions, we can change our way of thinking, and we can make a difference, not only in the lives of others, but also in the world around us.

Wisdom comes in knowing what belongs in each of the two piles. The radical acceptance comes in having the courage to own our power and to change what is ours to change. It comes in accepting that, no matter how much we'd like certain situations and people to be different, we simply don't have that power.

What we do have is an Inner Magnificence that invites us to live joy-filled lives, that invites us to stop frustrating ourselves. It makes available to us the wisdom to know which battles are ours to fight and which we need to let go. If you're having trouble deciding, here's a hint: you can't change anybody else; neither can you change anything that happened in the past.

So, here's my invitation for today: **Radically accept what is, right now, this moment. Let go of all expectations you have of how** you think things *should be,* and then have the courage to claim your power to change what is yours to change.

When you accept this in a radical way, you'll move into your Magnificence and be able to say, "I feel good about being me!"…and that's a promise.

Self-talk

L ast week at Sunday celebration, the minister was talking about the power of your word, and the use of affirmations to help us think positive thoughts and create a positive life experience for ourselves. She suggested that we create an affirmation and repeat it first thing in the morning, in the middle of the day, and finally just before we go to sleep. That's fine, but the real question is, what are the thoughts we are thinking the rest of the day? If we repeat our affirmation three times a day, and then three hundred times a day we think about how unpleasant our life is, where is the power of the affirmation?

Patrick Harbula, author of *The Magic of the Soul*, suggests a practice of, every night before we go to sleep, taking a rough inventory of what percentage of our day we spent thinking about our problems and what percentage we've spent thinking about how we want our life to be. He says that when we get our ratio up to seventy percent of our thinking and self-talk being about what we want our life to be instead of what we are currently experiencing, change begins to happen. That's when the creative power takes over. That's when what we are wanting begins to show up, and "the problem" begins to resolve itself.

The good news is that we are creators. The good news is that we are each authors of our own life story. The issue revolves around how we use our creative power.

Affirmations are wonderful tools, but their power is limited by how often we focus on them as compared to how often we focus on our current situation.

What is the story we tell ourselves about our lives? What percentage of the time do we spend thinking about all the reasons to be grateful for what we have in our lives, as compared to the percentage of time we think about all the things that we wish were different?

There seem to be four areas of our lives which can be the source of joy—or not. They are our financial situation, our relationships, our work, and our health. As we think about each of these aspects of our lives, know that we have an Inner Magnificence which is always wanting us to experience love, joy, goodness, health, abundance, and meaning in our lives.

So, here's my invitation for today: **Let most of your thoughts be positive or, as Paul says in his letter to the Philippians (4:8), "Finally, brothers [and sisters], whatever is true, whatever is honorable, whatever is just, whatever is pure, whatever is lovely, whatever is commendable, if there is any excellence, if there is anything worthy of praise, think about these things."**

The extent to which you do is the extent to which you'll be able to say, "I feel good about being me!"…and that's a promise!

Two Dollars

I was in a local supermarket the other day, standing in the "under fifteen items" line. There were two people in front of me: a middle-aged man in the process of paying for his order and an older man with items in his hand. As the first man was preparing to leave, he noticed that the man directly in front of me had dropped a dollar bill on the floor.

He called attention to it a couple of times before the older man realized what he had done. I saw that he put the two items he had on the conveyor belt. After picking up his dollar, he turned to me with a smile and held up a second dollar bill, rubbing the two together. "This is all I've got!" he said with a smile.

I was trying to quickly calculate whether two dollars would be enough to pay for his small order, and was already reaching into my pocket to have cash ready to make up whatever difference there might have been.

It turned out that my momentary generous spirit was unnecessary, as he had been very conscious of his resources and the cost of his purchase.

After paying, he turned back, smiled at me, and wished me a "Good Day!"

As I was walking to the parking lot afterwards, it occurred to me that I don't think I ever have been in the position of being in a grocery store with no credit card and only two one dollar bills as my total resource.

Two experiences came out of this for me:

1) However much this man had—or didn't have—in terms of available cash, it didn't affect his inner spirit. He smiled; he smiled appreciatively to the man who called attention to the money on the floor, he smiled at the clerk who scanned his two items and accepted his payment, he smiled at me. His happiness wasn't connected to money or things— it came from somewhere deep inside himself. It came from that Inner Magnificence, that Divine Spark that lives within all of us.

2) How incredibly blessed I am. I was at the market with the resources to buy anything and everything I wanted, let alone just what I needed. I was driving a reliable car, headed home to a house that we own, with a deck surrounded by flower boxes, overlooking a lush yard with trees and wetlands behind it, a patio table shaded by an off-set umbrella, a fire pit and a hot tub, and a wonderful wife, not to mention children and grandchildren of whom I am incredibly proud. I have my health and an abundance of friends.

Do I worry about money sometimes? Absolutely! Do I envy folks who have more? Without a doubt! Do I wish I had more financial resources, more financial freedom? Undeniably!

But here's the thing: Happiness always comes from the inside. Happiness isn't limited by what we have or don't have. It is about how we think about our circumstances.

So, here's my invitation for today: **Take time to count your blessings, no matter how much or little money is in your pocket! Count them! Count them all! The list is long!**

The extent to which you accept my invitation is the extent to which you'll be able to say, "I feel good about being me!"…and that's a promise!

When It Comes to Fixing People

She came to me because her husband has anger issues. He doesn't seem to trust her, and no matter how hard she tries, nothing seems to work. She came to me because she is frustrated that seemingly no matter what she does, she can't fix his anger.

In one incident she left the house, just to get away. She went to the nearby gas station to fill her tank and, just as she was about to pull away, he drove in and blocked her car at the pump.

She tried to talk calmly and asked him to let her out. She said she didn't want to make a scene. She didn't want to call the police. Inwardly, she was shaking in fear of what he might do next. That's just one of many stories of his anger she has experienced.

They have a history, and when things are good, they are *good!* She says that she loves him deeply, but she gets worn down by the angry outbursts.

In my years as a therapist, I've heard many versions of this story. One person has an "issue," and the other person is frustrated that they can't seem to fix their partner. Maybe the issue is anger, or addiction, or substance abuse, or their spending is out of control, or some other self-destructive behavior.

What I know is that trying to "fix" another person is a losing battle! We cannot change anyone; we cannot "fix" anyone. The most we can do is to love them. That means loving them enough to let them figure out their own lives—even if it means letting them go. It means loving them enough to let them experience the consequences of their behavior.

What we CAN do is to love ourselves enough to let go of unhealthy relationships, no matter how appealing they might seem to be.

What happens is that we love what we perceive to be the potential, instead of honestly looking at the reality of the situation, the situation that, no matter what we've tried, doesn't seem to be changing in a significant way.

Allowing someone to experience the consequence of their behavior is called "tough love," because it is tough to watch someone we love make self-destructive choices. It is tough to let go of a relationship that, when it is good, it is really good. It is tough to let go of the dream of what it might be like IF only the other person would change and be the way we want them to be. It is tough to deny ourselves the opportunity to grow into our best self when we are focusing so much energy on fixing them.

So, here's my invitation: **Move into your Magnificence and stop trying to get them to change their ways. Love yourself—and love them—enough to take a step back. Let them work out their own issues, whatever they might be. In the meantime, love yourself enough to follow a path that is filled with joy, a path that is fulfilling, a path that is filled with other people who take responsibility for healing their own pain. Let go of any need you have to "fix" and replace that with a desire simply to love, both them and you!**

The extent to which you do is the extent to which you'll be able to say, "I feel good about being me!"…and that's a promise!

Who You Were

I recently attended an event at Bryant University and was having lunch with several people, all with some connection to Bryant. As the conversation progressed, two of them realized that they were both Bryant alumnae from twenty-five or so years ago. As they talked more, they figured out that they lived in dorms next to each other. As they continued to search for connections, one of them said, "Oh, NOW I remember who you were!"

I think that hit a nerve in me. I wasn't sure how I would react to having someone remember who I _was._ Of course, it is usually flattering when somebody remembers us, but I don't think I want to be remembered for who I was. I want to be acknowledged for who _I am!_

When I look back over my life, there are some things that I am proud of and things that—in retrospect—are humiliating. Those aren't what I want to be remembered for. I don't want to be locked into and limited by _who I was._

Sure, there are lots of things about myself that are the same now as decades ago, and there are obvious differences. But I know that in some fundamental ways, I am not the person today that I was then. I have come a long way since then. I know I am a much better human being now, and am proud of how far I have come in my behavior and in my thinking.

What about you? How do you want to be remembered? Do you want to be remembered for the person you were, or the person you are?

The other side of that is how do you remember others? When you think back decades ago, do you remember them for the person they were back then, or are you open to getting to know the person they are now? To what extent do you hold someone's past against them, and to what extent can you allow for the possibility for change and accept them for who they are now?

Maybe another question is the extent to which you still beat yourself up for being who you were in your past and to what extent can you accept that that was then, and this is now?

Bryan Hubbard, in his book, *The Untrue Story of You*, suggests that we all have a past, we obviously have a present and, more importantly, we have a potential. I want people to think of me as who I am in this present moment, and to see my potential. We all have an Inner Magnificence, even though sometimes there are parts of our past when our lives were less than "magnificent."

As for me, I want to be seen for who I am, not limited by or remembered just for who I was.

So, here's my invitation: **The next time you get to reminiscing—either about your past or someone else's—choose to see the good and choose to see the potential. Embrace who you are in the present and get to know others for who they are in the present.**

The extent to which you do is the extent to which you'll be able to say, "I feel good about being me!"…and that's a promise!

Victories and Vices

Asking the Right Question

I'm not a hoarder, but I sure do keep a lot of "stuff!" We live in a relatively small house and it is full of stuff. My wife started out with a nice, neat "Barbie Doll" house, and then "Ken" moved in and brought a lot of his stuff. Not long afterwards my mother passed away and I brought more stuff as we emptied her home and got it ready to sell.

Shortly after that, my father-in-law moved from his home to join his wife at a nursing home, and that's when my wife brought a bunch of stuff from her parents' house. In the meantime, I have continued to acquire more stuff.

We had a consultant come in and evaluate our use of space and, after walking from room to room, moving from one floor to another, she paused and said, "Have you thought about getting a bigger house?" We laughed and told her that we already had a storage shed we were renting because when I first moved in, there already wasn't enough room in our house for all my stuff!

Probably the two biggest weaknesses I have are books and tools. I've given away box after box of books that I've accumulated over the years, each one a painful parting. Books, to me, are like friends—there is comfort in having them around! And as for tools, my thinking is that you can never have too many!

Every time I resolve to go through my stuff and get rid of some of it, I side-track myself with one or the other of two thoughts: 1) I might need this someday, or 2) I have an emotional connection with this.

I came across a book called *Spark Joy* by Marie Kondo, and from that I learned that I need to be asking a different question: "Does this item bring me joy?" I've been asking "Do I want to get rid of this?"

I know that I have too much stuff. I know we've long since run out of storage space, and we have made the decision not to get a larger storage unit. As a matter of fact, I've been talking for years about getting rid of the one we have, but it continues to attract more stuff.

The question isn't whether I can easily let something go, because there is so much I've kept! When I look at something, when I hold something, the more empowering question is whether it gives me the feeling of joy. I gave my high school and college year books to my children with the instructions to look through them—or not—and then throw them away. I finally let go of a complete thirteen volume set of the Interpreter's Bible; no library wanted them either! That information is all online now. I've also given away tools; how many hammers can I use? Letting go was painful, but hanging on wasn't giving me joy.

Isn't that a great guideline for life? Let go of anything that doesn't bring Joy!

What is in your life that you are hanging on to, even though there is no joy in it? What are you hanging on to just in case? What are you hanging on to because you "ought to?"

We each have an Inner Magnificence that is already complete, that needs nothing else, that wants us to know Joy in every aspect of our lives, but all too often we bury our Magnificence under lots of stuff.

So, here's my invitation for today: **Pick three things that are taking up space in your life, three things that don't bring you Joy**

and get rid of them. If you're courageous, do it again tomorrow and the next day until all you have is a JOY-full life!

The extent to which you do is the extent to which you'll be able to say, "I feel good about being me!"…and that's a promise!

Cheap

Some time ago we bought a bird feeder that has a built-in squirrel guard. It was a high-end feeder with an adjustable spring fastened to the perch so that if extra weight was on the perch, it would pull down a metal covering, making the food inaccessible. We used it to keep starlings and squirrels from consuming all the feed, allowing only smaller, lighter birds access.

After years of being in the weather, it broke, but it had come with a life-time guarantee. I returned it to the store where I had purchased it and, as soon as the store owners examined it, I noticed a disapproving look, followed by a mild rebuke that I had been using cheap birdseed. I remembered when I originally bought it they tried to sell me some of their birdseed, but I knew I could get birdseed much more cheaply at other outlets, so I took the least expensive way out and consistently purchased the cheaper birdseed.

The store owners explained how they could tell that I had gone that route. The inside of the feeder was covered with dust; quality birdseed is clean and doesn't leave dust residue. They explained that it was false economy. I learned that the feed I had been using had lots of "filler," seeds that the birds don't eat, but toss on the ground, and ground corn also to add bulk.

Deciding that they were giving me an education about bird feed, as well as a sales pitch, when they replaced my damaged feeder I bought the more expensive birdseed. I must admit that it actually lasts longer in the feeder. Birds aren't wasting it; there is much less on the ground.

This got me to wondering where else in my life am I taking the "cheap" way out, telling myself I am a smart buyer, rather than paying more for better quality. I do enjoy bargains and sales, and take satisfaction in finding them, but at what price?

I am thinking now about the food that I purchase. Sure, I can buy comparable items for less money, but am I depriving myself of healthier choices? Am I satisfied making a bad trade, under the guise of being economical? A similar thing happened to my wife and me with a swivel, rocker reclining chair we bought about five years ago. We bought a lower-end chair and told ourselves that we were getting a bargain. A couple of weeks ago, our bargain chair died. It is broken beyond repair, and of course the warranty has expired. On top of that, the chair needed to be reupholstered. Did we really save money when we bought the original chair? Probably not. We just got a cheaper chair, and here we are, already in need of buying another one.

In shopping for a new chair, we paid a good bit more, but it has a life-time warranty on moving parts, and we were told that we could expect the upholstery to last four to six times longer.

I remember a piece of advice from my dad: "You never save money buying cheap tools!"

Our Inner Magnificence is royalty at its finest. It deserves to be surrounded by quality.

So, here's my invitation: **Whether it is birdseed or groceries, furniture or tools, or anything else in life, choose quality over price.** That's a decision you'll never regret.

The extent you do is the extent to which you'll be able to say, "I feel good about being me!"…and that's a promise!

The Clearance Rack

I couldn't help laughing at myself. I went to Walmart (yes, I do shop at Walmart) for two things, just two things. I don't even remember now what they were, but on the way in, I noticed a sidewalk sale. Great bargains!

Always looking for a bargain, I went over and started going through all the miscellaneous merchandise to be liquidated. Sure enough, I found some really good buys, picked them up, and then went into the store to get the original two items.

Now I was walking back to my car with several items, several of which I didn't even know I needed until I saw them on the clearance racks outside the store.

I do the same thing with the Harbor Freight catalogue when it comes. I have a weakness for tools, and in the catalogue I might find a tool I don't yet know I need. A guy can never have too many tools. (The truth is that I probably already do.) I have tools I've used once or twice, tools I haven't used for decades. Some tools I have just in case I might be faced with a task that would make them useful.

I seriously doubt that I am the only person who has these kinds of thoughts. So, what is it about bargains that is so compelling? Yours might not be tools. It might be clothes, or QVC, or...???

If I am deeply honest, I think it has to do with some sort of inner emptiness. We are looking for something that will make us feel more complete, happier if only for a few minutes.

What we don't realize, or what we forget, is that we already have everything we need to make us happy. It is never material possessions that quench this thirst. What we desire is something less tangible. Fundamentally, our happiness depends on our own sense of gratitude for what we already have. Our happiness is contingent on an awareness of the riches the universe has already bestowed on us. It is a conscious realization of how good our life already is, and that goodness has almost nothing to do with things on sale or in a catalogue.

The next time you are tempted by a really good bargain, take a second and remind yourself of the riches you already have. Be honest about the difference between wants and needs.

My invitation is for us **to get in touch with our own inner wisdom and value who we are instead of what we have.**

The extent to which you accept my invitation is the extent to which you'll be able to say, "I feel good about being me!"…and that's a promise.

P.S. If you happen to run into me at a sidewalk bargain sale somewhere, feel free to remind me of how good my life already is, and there is nothing there I need!

Do You Want Fries with That?

The irony was not lost on me as I sat there eating my quarter-pounder with cheese, excitedly reading the newest addition to my library: *The Overnight Diet*. Oh, and yes, I did have fries with that!

What was the "hunger" I was feeding?

I couldn't help but think of the words of the Apostle Paul in his letter to the Romans, "For I do not do the good I want to do, but the evil I do not want to do—this I keep on doing." That might be a little harsh; I don't necessarily see eating a cheeseburger as evil (though some might!). I see it as a choice that is inconsistent with what I tell myself is my goal: losing weight and making healthy choices when it comes to food.

Honestly, who among us is not a member of this club? I think I'm not alone in wanting a quick fix to a problem without a substantial change in our habits and preferences.

We know what we need to do, or at least what we *say* we want, but then our behavior demonstrates something completely contrary.

Ernest Holmes teaches that it is our *dominant thoughts* that create our reality. When anyone looks at me, it is easy to see that my dominant thought has to do with eating for pleasure as opposed to eating for health. All the diet books in the world are not going to do anything for me, except maybe distract me from going within and getting a deeper understanding of what is controlling my behavior as I put food in my mouth. When do I eat? What do I eat? How much do I eat? How often do I eat? Why do I eat?

Honest awareness and answers to *these questions* will do much more for me in terms of creating a physically healthy body than reading **all** the diet books in the world.

I need to play with understanding what is behind all the food choices I make so that my behavior is consistent with what I say I truly want.

How about you? Where in your life do you see the irony between your behavior and what you tell yourself you want to experience?

To what extent are we controlled by our impulses as opposed to our commitment to living a healthy life? Are we driven by "hungers" and "thirsts" for the truly nourishing, or are we controlled by some unmet emotional need that lingers just beneath our conscious awareness?

We have in Inner Magnificence, an inner guidance system that wants only the best for us. It brings to our awareness the changes we need to make. It even helps us laugh at ourselves when our thoughts and behaviors don't match.

What will it be? Will you join me in being honest with yourself and commit to doing what you know is in your best interest, or will you be satisfied simply wishing your life was different, better?

So, here's my invitation for today: **Instead of mindlessly shoving food into your mouth, instead of habitually sipping from that glass or bottle, make a commitment to be mindful. Make a commitment to allow your actions to be consistent with supporting a healthy mind and body.**

The extent to which you accept my invitation is the extent to which you'll be able to say, "I feel good about being me!"...and that's a promise!

Doing Your Best or Getting By?

I remember as a student how, on group projects, some of my group members would be heavily invested in getting a good grade, and other members would be glad that somebody else was invested in getting a good grade. In other words, some members would do their best, and others would be along for the ride.

As a professor, I address this phenomenon of "social loafing" by having each group member anonymously give each other a participation grade. The consequence is that not everyone in the group will necessarily receive the same grade.

To avoid any awkwardness of coming to class with a fellow group member whose participation you might have deemed of a lesser quality, these group presentation grades are not posted until after the Final Exam.

After reminding my class of this, I was astounded when one of the students raised her hand and asked, "If you don't post the Presentation Grade until after I take the final exam, how will I know how hard to study for the final?"

"Do your best!"

I had already had an emotionally-laden conversation with this student, and a few others in the class, about the low grades they had received on their latest paper. Many of the papers were embarrassingly deficient. The papers evidenced no evidence of proofreading and contained numerous incomplete sentences. Organizationally, they lacked any clear beginning, middle, or end. Many of the students seemingly simply sat down at their computer and wrote a stream of consciousness on their chosen topic until the minimum length was met, and then they stopped.

The students were incensed about their grades. Several of them seemed to have an attitude of entitlement: "If I complete the assignment, I deserve an 'A.'" I told them that I knew they were capable of much better work and offered the option of resubmitting their papers. Several of them took me up on my offer; the results were like the difference between night and day

I went on to talk about the importance of building their reputation, and how one of my goals for them is to have a reputation of always doing their best. I wanted more for them than to have a reputation that says, "Here's somebody who is looking to get by with the least amount of effort."

We all know what it is like to be tired and feel overworked; we know what it is like to feel a time-crunch and do a job just to get it done. We know when we've done our best, and when we've just done enough to get by. My experience tells me that when I simply do enough to get by, yes, there is relief in having completed the project or task, but there is no sense of gratification, no sense of fulfillment.

We have an Inner Magnificence that wants us to hold our heads high and feel proud of our work. It wants us to connect to that little child part of us that used to do the smallest thing and wanted the world to see, because we were proud.

So, here's my invitation for today: **Live from your Magnificence; live with the intention that, no matter what you do, you can be proud; live so that you can look back and know that you didn't just get by, you did the best you could! Let that be your reputation.**

The extent to which you do is the extent to which you'll be able to say, "I feel good about being me!"...and that's a promise!

Feelings, Feelings

Don't get me wrong. I'm not against alcohol. I like a glass of red wine on occasion. I also like the harder stuff. I probably like it too much, which is why I mostly stay away from it.

My observation is that we drink because we want to numb our feelings. The most common reason people tell me they drink is because alcohol helps them relax, and who doesn't like to relax? Where people create problems for themselves is when they use alcohol—or anything else—to cover up and avoid their feelings.

There are a couple of points I want to make today from my professional perspective:

1) Sometimes our feelings are troublesome, and we judge them, but there is no such thing as a wrong feeling! How many times have we heard people tell us, "You shouldn't feel that way!" Well, whether I "should," or "shouldn't," I do. Feelings do not have a morality attached to them. Some are pleasant, and some are painful, but none of them are wrong. Feelings are simply information our body is generating.

- Admittedly, actions do have morality attached to them. There are right and wrong actions that can be triggered by our feelings. Feelings themselves, however, are simply feelings. As such, they come and go, and they change.

2) The purpose of our feelings is to provide us with information, and it is to our advantage to stop and gather the information our feelings can provide us, instead of using something (alcohol, food, shopping, sex, etc.) to escape the feelings.

   - So, if we're experiencing feelings that aren't pleasant, that is simply our body inviting us to move into our Magnificence and make a change, either in our behavior or, more often, in the way we are thinking about a situation.

I hear people tell me that sometimes they've had "one of those days," and they just want a drink. Before you pour yourself one, I would invite you to examine what you are feeling: tired, overwhelmed, angry, anxious, uncomfortable, or any one of a list of dozens more adjectives.

Could it be that you are not making good lifestyle choices, or that you're in a relationship that isn't working, or that your job isn't fulfilling? If that is the message, then all the alcohol in the world isn't going to change anything, unless it kills you, or gets you divorced or fired. The "solution" (pun intended) is to address the problem, not numb the feelings. When you're angry, maybe your boundaries have been violated and you need to reinforce them. Maybe your stress comes from unrealistic expectations, such as trying to make something work that isn't workable. If you are anxious, maybe that is your body inviting you to look within and discover the amazing inner strength hidden deep inside, strength you don't realize you have.

We all have an Inner Magnificence that wants only the best for us, and the primary way it communicates with our conscious self is through the creation of feelings, of emotions. I'm not saying, "Don't drink!" I'm saying don't cut yourself off from valuable biddings from life.

So, here's my invitation for today: **Feel your feelings, all of them. Be curious. Listen, and learn the lesson they want for you. It could be either to change your circumstances or to change your thinking, so that you can move into a life of passion, purpose, and joy.**

The extent to which you do is the extent to which you'll be able to say, "I feel good about being me!"…and that's a promise!

I Did It Again

I have a "thing" for books. I surround myself with them. Despite having purged myself of box after box of books, accumulated over decades. It is painful to give them away, even when I know they are going to good homes.

Years ago, my son challenged me to get rid of two books for every new book I acquire. I suspect he had the foresight to know that whatever I don't get rid of now, he and his sister will have to dispose of eventually.

I'm especially bad when it comes to traveling. I ALWAYS take many more books than I will ever read, even though I pack with the best of intentions. On a recent trip to the west coast, I knew there would be time on the plane, time between flights, and time at night after my meetings. My backpack of books was probably heavier than my suitcase, which contained enough clothes to last for a week!

I had crammed so many books into my backpack that it would hardly fit under the seat, as airline rules require. I don't travel with little books; I manage to talk myself into taking the big fat ones.

Getting a Kindle or Nook won't work, or so I tell myself, because so many of the books I'm interested in don't come in e-format, although this may change. I also feel a bit resentful in having to purchase e-book editions of books I've already paid for as hard copies. Another issue is that I'm a hands-on kind of guy. I like holding a real book in my hands; I like turning pages, not flicking my finger on a screen.

Like my eyes at an all-you-can-eat buffet, I chose way more than I read and, in doing so, sentenced myself to lugging an incredibly full and heavy back pack through one airport after another.

After each trip, I resolve to do it differently the next time, but when the next time comes, I yield to my passion for books and unnecessarily burden myself.

All of this got me to thinking about whether I do this in other areas of my life also, dragging a lot of unnecessary stuff along on my life's journey.

How about you? Do you needlessly encumber yourself with stuff that makes your journey through life more difficult than it needs to be? Maybe you carry with you a list of past hurts and resentments. Maybe you surround yourself with tangible items that you haven't allowed yourself to let go of. Maybe you have a habit that holds you back from the freedom you'd like to enjoy.

If you can identify, then here's my invitation for you: As painful, as challenging as it might be in the moment, **choose to lighten your load; leave some stuff behind. Choose to travel lightly through life. Claim your Inner Magnificence!**

The extent to which you do is the extent to which you'll be able to say, "I feel good about being me!"…and that's a promise!

100% Committed

If I had a dollar for every time I told myself that I need to cut sugar out of my diet, I'd be a *very* wealthy man. On some level, I know it isn't good for me. I know that it isn't good for my brain. I know that, if it had to choose, my brain would rather I consume fat. I also understand that our bodies need sugar because sugar gets converted to energy. However, I am walking testimony to the fact that the consumption of excess sugar causes our bodies to store it in the form of fat. I, for one, am walking around with an excess of "stored energy."

I jokingly say, "If it has frosting, it's for me!" I have a seemingly insatiable sweet tooth, and although I know it isn't good for me, I absolutely do enjoy the taste!

I tell myself I've made up my mind; I'm going to cut down. But how can I measure "cut down?" I know all about "SMART" goals: Specific, Measurable, Achievable, Realistic, and tied to a specific Timeframe.

I tell myself that I'm going to cut out all sugary desserts. Then I start thinking: Thanksgiving is coming up, and I don't want to deprive myself of desserts at Thanksgiving. And then, Christmas is coming, and who wants to skip desserts at Christmas? Then I make a New Year's resolution, but then Valentine's Day is on the horizon. You see the pattern, don't you?

I never quite commit 100% to stop. I'm always giving myself an out, an excuse to cheat.

I know that whatever goal we set for ourselves, whatever behavior we know we need to change, to be truly successful, we need to commit 100%, not 90%, not 95%, not 99%, not even 99.9%! We are either 100% committed or we aren't.

How would you like to be married to someone who is 95% committed to the marriage, or even 99.9%? Just like we don't want a partner who isn't 100% committed, neither will we be completely successful with any aspect of our life until we are willing to commit 100%. Even then, it doesn't always work out, but without the commitment, our success is doomed.

What is the behavior you need to change? What is it that you need to stop doing, or start doing? What is it that, if you followed through, would significantly change your life for the good? Is it making consistently wise choices with food? Is it stopping an addictive behavior? Is it setting money aside for a rainy day, or for retirement, or to help our children with paying for a college education? Is it the language you use around your children?

We have an Inner Magnificence that wants the best for us, but it requires us to be committed to experiencing our best selves.

Whatever the change is that we know we need to make, here's my invitation: **Move into your Magnificence and decide to be 100% committed, no wiggle room, no justifiable cheats. Whatever in your life is important, be all in! We either are committed 100%, or we aren't.**

The extent you are is the extent to which you'll be able to say, "I feel good about being me!"...and that's a promise!

Rewards

Yesterday, I stopped by the accountant with all the signed papers for our taxes to be e-filed, wrote the checks to both the state and the IRS for what we owed, and dropped them in the mail. I felt good. I had a sense of accomplishment. I got that out of the way for another year. I wanted to celebrate, to reward myself for a job well-done!

There's nothing wrong with that. We all like to reward ourselves for accomplishing something "big." The challenge for me is that the first thing I think about is sugar, frosting in particular. All I could envision was a nice, big, chocolate-frosted coffee roll! My mouth watered as I thought about all the frosting, with extra sugar. How good—ahem—bad could it be!

I tortured myself with the thought of that coffee roll for what seemed like an eternity. On one hand, I intellectually know that sugar is bad for me and, on the other hand, I know it tastes really good!

After all, I did deserve it, right?

But that isn't the issue, is it? It isn't about what I might or might not deserve, it is about whether it is ultimately in my best interest. I checked it out: 19 grams of fat, 18 grams of sugar, 430 mg of sodium, and 400 calories!

I know about the sugar addiction. I have it, and it's a tough one to break, as are all addictions!

I ended up coming home and eating a tangerine. It was sweet, juicy, but not nearly as satisfying. It was, however, a much healthier choice!

So often we choose to indulge in a behavior that we know isn't in our overall best interest, and we justify it by telling ourselves that we deserve it. I used to the do same things in Weight Watchers. I'd go to a meeting, hit my goal, and celebrate by picking up a cake on the way home.

My father-in-law once acknowledged that, until he met me, he had never known someone who could find so many excuses to have a cake! You know the momentous occasions, like the one-week anniversary of spring. I can be very creative in finding excuses to indulge my addiction.

It goes back to Freud's personality theory of the Id, the Ego, and the Super Ego. The Id is the part of us that wants us to feel good, to do what is fun in the moment. The Super Ego is the part that reminds us what is in our ultimate best interest, and the Ego is like the judge who hears both sides and makes the call on which part wins. Therapy, for Freud, was having his patients learn to increase their Ego strength and not be either so impulsive that they always do what they feel like, nor so rule-bound that they can't have fun and enjoy themselves.

So, what about you? Which inner voice do you pay attention to: the one that says, "Do it! You'll like it!" or the one that says, "This really isn't in your best interest."

Here's my invitation: **The next time you want to reward yourself for a good job, well done, choose something that will be for your ultimate good.** Let your Inner Magnificence have the deciding vote.

The extent to which you do is the extent to which you'll be able to say, "I feel good about being me!"…and that's a promise!

Swallowing Frogs

I guess it got lost along the way, but I used to have a sign above my desk, a quote attributed to Mark Twain, that read: "If you have a frog to swallow, don't look at it too long; and, if you have more than one frog to swallow, swallow the biggest one first!"

Now, I've never really swallowed a frog, unless eating frog legs counts, but in that case, they were no longer alive, they were seasoned, cooked, and tasted like chicken. However, I have, on occasion, had a day in which I faced some unpleasant task—really unpleasant. Maybe I had to let an employee go, an employee who I really liked, but one that was not performing to the level required by the job. Maybe it was the need to respond to a student about why they received a failing grade on a paper that they thought was great. Maybe it was about confronting a person about—what I considered to be—their inappropriate behavior.

You get the gist. I doubt there are any of us who haven't faced an unpleasant task and put it off, because it is *unpleasant.* There are tasks that we put off, I guess hoping that somehow they will go away or take care of themselves, but they never do. They just hang there, waiting for us to act.

The truth is that no matter how long we put off the unpleasant task, it isn't going to become any easier. Equally true is the great relief we experience once we have done it, once we've addressed it. Even when the results might not be what we had hoped for, even though the encounter may have ended on an unpleasant note, at least it was done! An emotional weight was lifted, and we felt better.

We have an Inner Magnificence that wants us to feel good about our lives, that wants us to squeeze as much joy as we can into each day. This Magnificence will give us the strength and courage to do what needs to be done so we can get past the unpleasantness and move on to the relief.

What happens to a lot of us is that, instead of trusting ourselves and our Inner Magnificence, we put off the unpleasantness, and prolong the discomfort by thinking about how unpleasant the task seems.

Susan Jeffers, author of the best-selling *Feel the Fear, and Do It Anyway,* has a slogan: "No matter what happens, I can handle it!" Imagine what it would be like to look at the frog and remind yourself that, no matter what happens, you can handle it!

Here's my invitation for today: **Stop putting off those unpleasant tasks; stop avoiding those tasks that, the longer you look at them, the more overwhelming they feel. Go ahead, stop looking at the frog and swallow it! Believe that your Inner Magnificence has got your back and there is nothing that you, through it, can't handle! And, if you have several frogs to swallow, go ahead and swallow the biggest one first!**

The extent to which you do is the extent to which you'll be able to say: "I feel good about being me!"...and that's a promise!

What I Learned about Success from being a Failure

S everal years ago, I found myself in a transition time and was look-ing for a different job. I was recruited by a company to be an in-surance agent. The recruiting speech made it very appealing. There is a lot of money to be made. The bonuses were enticing. There is almost unlimited potential. So, I got my license, went through the ori-entation training, and jumped in

By all measurements, after a little over a year, I had failed miser-ably. The compensation is solely commission based, and I felt like I was drowning. There were many days when it cost me to go to work, driving around the state at my own expense, having not made any sales. No one could understand because, from all appearances, I had everything it took to be successful. But none of that mattered. As far as income was con-cerned, I would have probably been better off working at McDonalds!

Since then, I've done a lot of research on what makes people successful. Albert Gray said that it boils down to one thing: Successful people do things that unsuccessful people aren't willing to do! In the insurance industry it is calling on people who don't want to see us and talking to them about something they don't want to talk about. I can remember my first week, sitting in the Conference Room, organizing my sales notebook instead of being on the phone trying to get appointments. Organizing my notebook was comfortable; calling people who didn't want to talk to me was uncomfortable! Few people I know enjoy spending the day trying to get appointments by calling people who don't want to talk to them. But that's the "secret" to success; you consistently do what is difficult!

To be successful in anything, you must be willing to do things that aren't easy, aren't natural, aren't pleasant. If you want to be successful in losing weight, you must make tough decisions about changing your lifestyle, your eating habits. If you want to be in better shape physically, you must make yourself uncomfortable by creating the habit of exercising on a consistent basis.

I've researched entrepreneurs and discovered that the successful ones do uncomfortable things daily. Attending a lot of meet-ups can be fun, but having a conversation with people, and asking for a response, and doing that day after day every day can be daunting.

What about you? What is it that you'd like to be successful doing, but aren't? It really does boil down to that old cliché: "Make it a habit to get out of your comfort zone," and do it every day!

We have an Inner Magnificence. We have inside us everything we need to be incredibly successful in every area of our life. We simply need to stop limiting ourselves by doing what is comfortable and follow through with the uncomfortable. Again, it was Albert Gray who said that "It is easier to adjust ourselves to the hardships of a poor living than it is to adjust ourselves to the hardships of making a better one."

Here's my invitation for today: Move into your Magnificence. **Think of one thing that, if you did it on a consistent basis, would make your life better, and do it, despite how uncomfortable you might feel.**

The extent you do is the extent to which you'll be able to say, "I feel good about being me!"...and that's a promise!

What Kind of Partner Am I?

F alling in love is easy; it just seems to happen. Staying in love can be tricky. How many times have I heard a client tell me, when talking about their partner: "I still love them, I'm just not 'in love' with them?" Sadly, most of the time those clients are looking for a justification to leave their current partner, rather than looking for ways to rekindle the spark.

What happened to that feeling of being head-over-heels in love? What allows so many to lose that sense of joy and connectedness?

Here's one of the puzzle pieces: There is a question and a thought and those are stuck in the deep recesses of the mind of my client: "Is there somebody else out there who would make a better partner than the one I have now?" and "I'm open to finding that 'someone better.'" This kind of thinking sets a person up to compare their partner with everyone they meet. These comparisons are bound to make us fall out of love, because we end up making comparisons between our real life and our fantasy life, and fantasy is always more appealing.

Instead of continuing to focus on all the reasons why we fell in love in the beginning, instead of thinking about all the qualities we appreciate in our partner, we begin looking at our partner's flaws. We catalogue those little (and sometimes big) irritating habits. We focus on our partner's perceived faults and, on a mostly unconscious level, we constantly scan our environment for somebody else who appears to be a much better match for us.

Instead of continuing to appreciate all the good qualities of our partner, and being grateful and appreciative every day, we look at the imperfections. Invariably, we will find someone without *those* flaws, and we perceive them as the "perfect" partner. We allow ourselves (once again) to be blinded by the excitement of the new connection, forgetting that there is no such thing as a *perfect* partner, deluding ourselves from the realization that we are just trading one set of imperfections for another.

Instead of wondering if there is a better partner somewhere out there, we—and our relationship—would be much better served if we wondered how we could *be* a better partner. When was the last time you asked your partner what you could do to make the relationship stronger and more satisfying for them?

Another factor that undermines our relationships is the unwillingness to be completely transparent. When considering doing something, we don't stop and ask, "How is this going to benefit my partner?" We keep secrets, thinking only about how WE might experience joy and find pleasure. We don't stop to think about how our partner would feel if they were to know all that we are doing. There are parts of our lives that we make off-limits for our partner and, by creating those barriers, we erode the feelings of connection and trust.

We have an Inner Magnificence which wants only the best for us, which wants us to experience all that is good and rich and joyous. Here's the catch: We can only connect with it by looking within; looking outwardly for it is a recipe for staying dissatisfied.

So, here are some invitations for you:

1) **every day, remember and express appreciation for the qualities that drew you to your partner in the first place;**

2) **every day, ask yourself how you could be a better partner; and**

3) **before you do *anything*, take into consideration how your partner would feel if they knew what you were about to do.**

The extent to which you accept this invitation is the extent to which your relationships will be stronger, and you will be able to say, "I feel good about being me!"…and that's a promise!

Nature and Culture

As Smart as Grass

I built a couple of raised garden beds this summer. There isn't anything better than enjoying fresh vegetables right out of your own garden.

After marking the layout, I began digging up the sod. It turned into a much more labor-intensive project than I had first anticipated. (Isn't that the way with almost every home improvement project?)

I would dig up a small piece of sod and then proceed to knock off as much dirt as I could, knowing that this was a great way to start; with a loose base on which I would eventually put fresh topsoil in the frame. With every piece of sod, I was struck by two things: what an amazingly intricate root system the grass had developed, and how deeply the roots had grown. It is as if the grass has an inherent wisdom, somehow knowing that if it is going to thrive, it needs to build a web beneath the surface that will maximize its opportunity to absorb nutrients and moisture, and the deeper the root structure, the less dependent it is on the surface water.

So, the question becomes: "Are we as smart as grass?" It's a humbling thought, don't you think? Do we consciously do what grass does inherently?

Do we intentionally grow deeper, searching for that which nourishes and makes us healthy, allowing us to reach our full potential, or are we satisfied with the superficial? If so, how does that support us in times of emotional drought?

How committed are we to practices that deepen our awareness of Truth and allow us to absorb wisdom that is deeper than a TV sound bite or someone's posting on Facebook? I know there are lots of posts of ancient wisdom on Facebook, but anybody who goes through Facebook with any degree of regularity—I know who you are!—knows that there are lots of opinions and postings that fail the "Is this really true?" test.

What if we spent as much time writing in a gratitude journal as we spend doing mindless things? What if we spent time meditating, discovering and nurturing our inner wisdom, instead of reacting to the fears and perspectives that are hyped by the news channels?

It seems to me that our lives would be so much richer and more fulfilling if we would refuse to accept the superficial, if we would tap into the depth of our own inner wisdom.

How far out and how far down do we reach for Truth, or do we simply absorb what the world puts in front of us each day? Do we take the time, do we make the effort to search for Truth, or do we limit ourselves to that which is shallow, easily accessible, and simply confirms our own biases?

My invitation for today is that you **go deeply within; get in touch with your Inner Magnificence. Be at least as smart as grass!**

The extent to which you accept my invitation is the extent to which you'll be able to say, "I feel good about being me!"…and that's a promise!

Avoiding the Trees

Some time ago we were visiting my son in rural West Virginia and he decided that it would be fun to get out his mini-bikes to ride. It DID sound like fun, though I hadn't ridden a motorcycle in years and I'd never been on a mini-bike. I had always ridden on pavement and never off-road. He has a big yard, and part of it is populated with some large trees.

He went through the instructions about the brake and the throttle and then had one last piece of advice: "When you see the trees, always look at where you want to go; don't look at what you want to avoid!"

This is a profound piece of advice. We tend to move in the direction of what we are looking at, whether we're riding mini-bikes or living life.

When I encourage people to create affirmations for themselves, I *always* tell them to create positive affirmations. Affirm what you are wanting, not what you are wanting to avoid. There is something in our imagination that doesn't register negative qualifiers.

My son was wise in not saying, "Whatever you do, don't hit the tree!" The image in my mind would have been one of hitting the tree, the very thing I wanted NOT to do! By keeping my focus on where I want to go—into the open spaces—that's the image I have: seeing myself

161

easily weaving through the openings and experiencing the joy of the ride.

Wherever you are in life, I am sure that there are some things you want to achieve and there are some things you want to avoid. Focus on what you want to achieve—don't give space in your imagination for that which you want to avoid.

Imagine the experiences in life that would bring you joy. Keep out any thoughts of fear or disaster, any thoughts of events and circumstances that only serve to stir up anxiety, leaving you in a state of unease or concern.

Paul, in his letter to the Philippians, says it well: "Whatsoever things are true, whatsoever things are honest, whatsoever things are just, whatsoever things are pure, whatsoever things are lovely, whatsoever things are of good report; if there be any virtue, and if there be any praise, think on these things."

When riding the mini-bike, relatively speaking, there were LOTS of open spaces and a few trees. The joy was in focusing on the open spaces I wanted to enjoy; the potential for disaster would have been in focusing on the trees I didn't want to hit!

As you go through your day today, here's my invitation: **Don't think about the "trees" you don't want to run into, but focus instead on the joy of easily steering into the open spaces of your dreams!**

The extent to which you accept my invitation is the extent to which you'll be able to say, "I feel good about being me!"…and that's a promise!

Be the Light

If you put up a Christmas tree, when do you take it down? There are lots of traditions around putting up and taking down Christmas decorations. When I was little, Santa brought the tree and the presents. I don't really remember when we took it down. I know some people take down their tree the day after Christmas. They put it up the weekend following Thanksgiving, and they're ready for it to go! Some people take down their tree on New Year's Day: out with the old, in with the new. Others wait until January 6th, Epiphany, in honor of the Twelve Days of Christmas—the time between when, as tradition has it, Jesus was born, and the Wise Men got to the stable to honor him.

We usually take ours down sometime the first week of January. Each year, when we take it down, I miss it! Yes, this year, I thought we had an especially pretty tree, but every year, after the tree is down and the lights are gone, there is an emptiness for me.

I like those quiet times just before bed, when the TV is off and only the Christmas tree lights are shining. There is something peaceful about it; there is a different kind of light in the room.

I do like the order that returns to the house when all the decorations are down and put away for another year. The furniture goes back to its usual place. My wife and I go back to our normal routines—whatever that means—and we start to look forward to warmer weather. But I miss the lights.

There is something primal about light. It doesn't matter whether our trees have all white lights or colored lights; it doesn't matter whether they are larger bulbs or the smaller twinkling ones. To me, the light they emit represents warmth and peace and beauty.

So, when the Christmas tree is gone, I have to look elsewhere. Maybe that is it: When the tree is up, the lights are there, but without the tree I have to look, and that takes effort. Without the effort, without the intention, I simply allow myself to get caught in the dark days of winter.

How about you? Where do YOU look to see light during the dark winter months? I'm not talking about regular lights; I'm talking about the light that makes you smile. I'm talking about the light that causes you to feel peace and joy, warmth and love. You know, like the sparkle in someone's eyes, the smile on a child's face, or the kind gesture of a stranger.

I know that within each of us is a light, our Inner Magnificence. Sometimes we allow it to get covered up; sometimes we cover it up, as if to protect it, but it is still there.

So, here's my invitation: **Let your light shine! Be the light in someone else's life. Cause someone's face to light up because you committed a random act of kindness or because you simply had a smile on your face.**

I started to say that I will if you will, but I'm going to do it whether you do or not, and the extent to which you allow the light of your true self to shine into someone else's life is the extent to which you'll be able to say, "I feel good about being me!"…and that's a promise!

Deadheading

P art of my ritual of watering the planter boxes on our deck is to "deadhead" the geraniums. In early spring, we have pansies in a planter near the front door of our house, and pretty much every time I come home, and my hands aren't already full, I will stop and deadhead the pansies, picking the flowers that are past their peak.

What I know is that this process of deadheading flowers is one that makes the plants healthier and prolongs their beauty. When the mature blooms are left alone to "go to seed," it signals the plant to stop growing, that it has ended its useful life, but when the old blooms are regularly removed, the plant becomes more vigorous, heartier, and produces more beautiful blooms.

Recently, as I was going about my routine, I realized the parallel for my own life. Every day, I have a choice to break off those experience from my past—no matter how beautiful they might have been—and allow myself room to grow and be more productive.

It is when we stop tending to our lives, when we hang on to the old ways of thinking, that we stop growing.

When I walk into the basement, I see all sorts of odds and ends that I have yet to be able to give myself permission to toss; when I walk into my office, I am surrounded by piles of papers and more books and magazines and articles that I tell myself have value, material that I "might" use someday.

I wouldn't call myself a hoarder (but others might take one look and disagree), but today I had one of those "Aha!" moments while tending the flowers, a moment that suggested I would do well to be diligent in, and get as much pleasure from, deadheading my life and my living space.

As I look around, I see so many things that, in their days, had their own beauty, so many things that seemed like treasures, but whose beauty has long since faded. Now they are simply taking up space.

Today, I'm also inviting you to take a close look at the garden in your mind. No doubt, some of what you find will be weeds, thoughts and beliefs that simply don't belong there at all.

Then there are those thoughts and beliefs that were once beautiful, but now have begun to stunt your growth. Here are a couple of examples: I once made the decision not to tell anyone what I was really feeling. It was a beautiful way of protecting myself from people making fun of me. Then there was that decision not to tell anyone what I really thought; again, this was a stunning way of protecting myself from ridicule.

The problem is that the longer I hold on to those beliefs, and make decisions based on them, the more I stunt my growth, the more isolation I create. Finding the courage to deadhead these beliefs and thought patterns that once served me well stimulates me to grow into a deeper and more powerful truth: that who I am—with thoughts and feelings that are expansive, rather than limiting— is my true beauty.

So, here's my invitation: **Move into your Magnificence. Connect with your potential rather than allowing yourself to be limited by your past. Deadhead all in your life which has lost its beauty and is hindering your growth.**

The extent to which you accept my invitation is the extent you'll be able to say, "I feel good about being me!"…and that's a promise!

It Pays to Listen

I attended a national Quantum Leap seminar, led by Steve Harrison, and he told a story about how he and his wife had gone to a charity auction and noticed several "offerings" which had no bids on them. Steve decided to sign up with a nominal bid, hoping that would entice others to also bid. At the end of the night, his wife excitedly told him that they had won…a morning of bird watching!

To say that Steve was less-than-excited would be an understatement. He and his wife went, and quickly realized that they were the only attendees! The guide was an older man who was extremely excited to finally have someone there to learn bird watching.

The guide started out saying, "Listen…that's a robin!" "Listen…that's a cardinal!" "Oh, listen…that's a scarlet tanager!" The guide gave the binoculars to Steve and pointed in the direction of the sound and, looking, he saw one of the most beautiful birds he had ever seen.

That's when Steve realized that "bird watching" is first about "bird listening."

As I thought about his story, it occurred to me that some of the most powerful experiences we have are the result of learning to listen, whether it is to our children, our friends, our colleagues, our employees,

167

or anyone. There is a deep connection that happens when we learn to listen, whether it is listening to nature, other people, or our own Inner Voice.

What we are truly listening, we have access to information which has the potential of being life-changing, both for the person who walks away feeling heard, and for us, because life really is about connecting with the world and all that is in it, including the people around us.

Listening, truly listening, listening to learn and learning to listen, is a powerfully transformative skill.

I can't begin to tell you how many clients I have had over the years who have come to me simply because they don't feel heard, either at home or at work or in the world. Admittedly, part of that has to do with how they talk, how they communicate. They use language that attacks, that demeans and judges. They talk incessantly because they aren't "listening" to the body language of the person with whom they are talking. The listener has "checked out" some time ago, and they're so into what they have to say that they don't even notice that the other person has stopped listening.

In an ironic way, they've set it up so that people don't listen because they've not developed the skill to listen to what their "audience" is communicating non-verbally.

Celeste Headlee, host of "On Second Thought," a show on Georgia Public Broadcasting, is convinced that **everyone** has something amazing to say when we learn to listen.

So, here's my invitation today: **Move into your Inner Magnificence and consciously practice listening, truly listening. Be prepared to be amazed at what you learn about the world around you and the people in it.**

The extent to which you do is the extent to which you'll be able to say, "I feel good about being me!"…and that's a promise!

The Garden

Yesterday's record setting temperature turned my attention to my garden beds and the need to care for them. Not only do they need to be watered, they're a mess. I have raised beds full of dirt, modestly covered by straw, but otherwise completely barren.

But looks can be deceiving. Yesterday I saw lettuce and tomatoes, squash and carrots, beans and spinach, flowers and peppers. I'm not hallucinating; I'm imagining. I'm visioning, as some would say.

Some people would see the mess, and I see it too, but I have made a point to also see the potential.

I wish I could do the same thing as easily with people as I can do with my garden, to see the potential instead of the mess.

Sometimes I CAN and do. Other times the judgmental part of me takes over. I judge by appearances, by outward behaviors. That's not one of my better qualities.

"Judge not, lest you be judged," the Bible says. "There, but for the grace of God go I," is also a quote that is often given biblical weight (though the exact origins of the idea are not clear).

This is a wonderful reminder that it is always worth the effort to look beyond the appearances and see the possibilities.

It is much easier to make quick judgments based simply on sensory input, but when we take the time to look for the potential, for the possibilities, how life changes! This is as true for people and life circumstances as it is for garden beds.

The next time you find yourself making a judgment about what life is presenting you, I extend the invitation to stop, acknowledge what you are experiencing, and then ask, "But what is the potential? What are the possibilities?"

Emma Curtis Hopkins was famous for her declaration, "There is Good here, and I demand to see it!"

I can do that with my garden. Despite the lack of anything green (except for a few weeds), I know that beneath the soil are luscious vegetables. I simply need to be patient, and care for the garden. I know the potential in every one of the seeds I planted. Not only do I not need to do anything to the seeds, I can't do anything, except to keep the soil moist and keep the weeds at bay. The seeds will take care of turning my raised beds of dirt into a bountiful crop of wonderful vegetables.

When we learn to see the good, to see the possibilities, to see the potential in people and situations, we will have taken a big step into our Inner Magnificence. That's when we will demonstrate that our task is to provide an environment in which the potential becomes the reality.

If we can do it with a garden, we can do it with the people around us as well.

So, here's my invitation: **Move into Your Magnificence; instead of making judgments based on what is easily visible, look past the first impression and see the hidden potential.**

The extent to which you accept my invitation is the extent to which you will be able to say, "I feel good about being me!"...and that's a promise!

It's Always There

New Englanders talk a lot about the weather. For several days lately it's been cold, overcast, rainy with a wind that is piercing. It has been dreary and miserable. Somebody joked the other day, asking what that bright yellow ball was in the sky.

What is challenging to remember when we are complaining about the dreariness, is that the yellow ball in the sky was there all the time. It never went away; it was just covered up by clouds.

What if we had a magic machine that could cut through the cloud cover, that could allow the sun to shine through, that could allow the warmth and light to be present in our experience whenever we wanted it?

While we haven't figured out the science for that yet, the Law of Attraction talks about a "mental equivalent." For everything in the physical world, there is an equivalent inner experience. There is the sun in our solar system and there is a light within each of us that gives off warmth and light and love. Within each of us is a source of goodness and joy that never goes away. The challenge is that our life circumstances and situations often seem to get in the way and block out that experience. At times, our life can seem dark, dull, cold, depressing, sad, meaningless, and empty.

171

It is my contention that within each of us there is a magic fountain which is constantly pouring Good into our lives, always! This fountain is oblivious to all the external circumstances. It never stops overflowing with Goodness, despite what we might be experiencing outwardly.

Too often, we allow the unpleasant experiences to get in the way and temporarily block out any awareness of this Good. The good news is that the fountain never stops gushing forth Good. The even better news is that we do have the ability to allow that into our lives whenever we choose!

While we can't necessarily control the circumstances in our lives, we do have control over that to which we give our attention.

Let's begin by making a list of the people and circumstances for which we can be sincerely grateful, the small blessings. It may be something as simple as being able to turn on a faucet and having clean water to drink. It may be remembering the people in our lives who love us even when we aren't acting very lovable. It may be having the ability to turn up the thermostat and feel the warmth. There are infinite experiences available to us every day that remind us of life's goodness, even amid the darkest times.

This isn't meant to deny the darkness and the pain. It is meant to be a reminder that, amid those experiences, there is always more; all we need to do is to allow ourselves to look for the joy, experience the gratitude, and feel the warmth.

So, here's my invitation for today: **Move into your Magnificence and consciously choose to look for the Good.** Like the sun, it's always there!

The extent to which you do is the extent to which you'll be able to say, "I feel good about being me!"…and that's a promise!

Nature Always Wins

Admittedly, I'm not a fan of modern art, but I recently toured the Hirshhorn Museum in Washington, DC. I was struck by one of the sculptures outside. It is a 1992 Chrysler Spirit that has been crushed by a nine-ton volcanic boulder, and the boulder has eyes and a mouth painted on it. The title of Jimmie Durham's piece is *Still Life with Spirit and Xitle*.

The artist is trying to convey the fundamental truth that nature always wins! We can work with nature, or against it, but ultimately, nature is going to win.

I sometimes enjoy watching a TV series about engineering disasters; this is a chronicle of things gone wrong because someone in the process overlooked or didn't respect the laws of nature.

When we work with nature, amazing things happen. Years ago, I designed and built a passive solar cabin, situated so that it was insulated by the earth on the north side. No sun ever came in directly from the east or west and sun only entered the cabin from its south side between the autumn and spring equinoxes. It was built on a concrete slab which absorbed the heat during the day in the winter and released it during the night, creating a thermal flywheel. The temperature could be in the thirties outside, but the inside of the cabin would be in the seventies, with no external heat source other than the sun.

How about you?

What choices are you making that will leave this planet a healthy place for our grandchildren and great grandchildren?

All this talk of wanting to save our planet is bogus, in my opinion. The planet is going to survive. The question is whether we will work with nature so that it continues to be hospitable to human life, or are we going to push it past that limit by our greed and our carelessness, making it a place where our children and grandchildren suffer from global warming and polluted air and water supplies?

The reality is that nature doesn't really care whether we exist on this planet or not. Nature is a powerful force. We can deceive ourselves into believing that somehow the laws of nature don't really apply to us. Our pride and arrogance can deceive us into thinking that someone will find a magic cure just in time, like in the movies, but, and I will again say: Nature always wins, just like the sculpture says!

So, here's my invitation to you: **Each day, decide to take a step and make your life more "green," more nature-friendly.** Maybe it is not to use plastic bags, or conserving water. Maybe it is recycling and composting. Maybe it is buying locally. The list is endless, but it starts with a personal commitment to work *with* Nature.

The extent to which you do is the extent to which you'll be able to say, "I feel good about being me!"…and that's a promise, one that will make Mother Nature smile!

Rethinking "Sweet"

Anyone who knows me knows my relationship with sweets. For those of you who don't know me, I have a very intimate relationship with them! My slogan is: "If it has frosting, it's for me!" Donuts (Krispy Kreme is the ultimate), pastries, and pretty much everything with frosting has my name on it.

While I should be rethinking my relationship with sweets, what I'm actually rethinking is my reaction to being called "Sweet!" As I have gotten older, it seems to happen with more frequency. I know! I know: It is meant to be a compliment. But, up until recently, I've cringed inwardly.

In my mind, sweet is an adjective that refers to little boys and girls who do something nice, something thoughtful, or something kind. But, I'm not a little kid anymore. Well, maybe part of me still is, but that's for another time.

My wife often comments on something I've done as "sweet." "You're so sweet!" "That was sweet of you!" I know she is well-intended, so I accept the compliment, but I want to say, "Stop saying that about me!" Call me kind, call me thoughtful. Call me *anything*—just don't call me sweet!

Then it happened with a friend after I complimented a photo of her. "That was so sweet," she said. Somehow, I've been taking comments like this as an assault on my manhood! Women are sweet; children are sweet. Men are–I don't know what–but not *sweet*!

So, what's with that?

Is my manhood really diminished when someone tells me that I've done something sweet? Why can't sweet be added to the list of attributes for masculinity? Or, do we just need to get away from those stereotypes for masculine and feminine behavior, and just talk about simple humanness?

Some people aspire to androgyny, combining the best of both genders. How is it that we've categorized some character traits as masculine and others as feminine? What if, instead of labeling or judging ourselves—or others—as being so masculine or so feminine, we just talked about what a great human being they are?

Maybe that's the task of our times: to stop thinking about the gender-appropriateness of labels that are used to describe us and think simply about whether our behaviors have made another person feel better, or worse, about themselves.

In terms of the food we eat, many of us, me especially, would be well-served to have fewer sweets in our diets. But, in terms of how we are treated and in terms of how we treat others, the world can use all the sweetness it can get!

So, here's my invitation for today: **Move into your Magnificence and do something sweet for somebody else...anybody else!**

The extent to which you do is the extent to which you'll be able to say, "I feel good about being me!"...and that's a promise!

Unintentional Consequences

For some time now, my wife and I have had a bird feeder on our deck. We thoroughly enjoy watching the activity and variety of birds that come. We have enjoyed this so much that recently we added two more feeders, one for thistle seed and one that holds a suet cake. In doing this, we have attracted a wider variety of birds and more beauty!

The sides of our yard are bounded by arborvitae bushes. Birds build nests there; they dart in and out on their forays to and from the feeder. These shrubs offered a degree of protection for the birds, or so we thought.

Last week, for the first time ever, we saw a hawk, perched on a tree branch in the wetlands behind our home. Two days later I watched the hawk land on the top of the shrubs, then dive into them I watched branches rustling; a few feathers emerged, and the hawk made its escape.

What started out as watching the peaceful beauty of nature, became a scene of the more violent aspect of nature. By providing feeding stations for smaller birds, we inadvertently provided a feeding station for raptors, carnivorous birds.

They, too, have their own beauty: their colors, their majesty, their gracefulness, their speed.

It is one thing to know about nature's food chain, but I don't like to watch it. I know some animals feed on other animals, but I don't like to watch it in my backyard.

In some ways, it is hypocritical. After all, I also eat meat. I just don't like to think about an animal needing to be harvested. I don't like to think about the violent part of that process, let alone participate in it, but I do enjoy a good steak and fried chicken.

There are a couple of lessons in this for me.

The first is that the unintentional consequence of creating an attraction for smaller birds has turned into having built a feeding station for larger birds that feed on the birds attracted to our feeder. I need to live with that or stop doing it!

The second is a reminder that I, too, am a predator on the food chain. I just don't like thinking about myself that way. I like to think about just going to the super market and picking out something nice to grill. I realize that I don't even like to go to a butcher shop; the name itself is a reminder of an animal being killed and butchered for my dining pleasure. I usually do my shopping at a supermarket. There's nothing violent about that image!

I'm not yet ready to give up eating meat, but this is a good reminder of how I participate in the bigger picture of life and death, at least in the animal world.

So, here's my invitation: **Be mindful of the implications of your choices, all of them.** Sometimes there are unintentional consequences, and sometimes there are implications that we'd rather not think about. Being mindful may not be pleasant, but the more honest we are with ourselves, the better we will feel about ourselves.

Live from your Inner Magnificence, which demands total honesty and transparency. The extent to which you do is the extent to which you'll be able to say, "I feel good about being me!"...and that's a promise!

The Best Kind of Service

Being Compassionate, Taken Advantage of, or Both

A s I was getting out of my car to fill my tank, a car pulled up on the other side of the same pump. The guy got out and caught my eye. He smiled, as if he recognized me. I was searching my own inner databank, trying desperately to locate him. At that point, he started a conversation with me. It was a story about how there was some personal crisis and he was on his way to Logan Airport to pick up somebody, it was late at night, and he stopped to fill his tank with gas and just realized that—in his haste to get to the airport—he left his wallet home in Westerly.

I listened, then cut him off and tried to sum up the situation: "So, you want money from me." He said, "I need gas…so yes, money or just put some gas in my car so I can get to the airport without the stress of possibly running out."

I have felt taken advantage of so many times by strangers' stories of hardship and my immediate reaction was to say, "Sorry, but I can't help you tonight!" But in my spiritual practices lately, I've been playing with the idea that between our reaction and our response is what Tracy

Balzer calls a "thin space." Our reactions are learned, often to protect us. But there is that space that we have before we react, giving us a second to think and choose.

This time, I did get into that "thin space," and thought about what it must feel like to be in the place of this stranger, in the midst of a challenging situation, desperate to get somewhere to meet somebody and to have been so distracted as to leave my money clip and driver's license at home, miles away. I could go back home and make myself over an hour late to meet my obligation, or humble myself to ask a stranger for help.

I pulled out my cash and gave him ten bucks, allowing him to buy at least enough gas to get to Boston. He thanked me profusely and said that he hoped I was having a better night than he was.

I drove away with my head spinning. Did I just get conned by a really good story or did I just take a bit of stress off a stranger? I will never know the answer, but here's where I trust the "law of circulation": What we give comes back to us.

I didn't do it so I would get something back. I did it because that's what I hope someone would do for me if the situation was reversed. And, if he was conning me, I wish he could know of his Inner Magnificence.

The point is that I responded instead of reacted. I gave myself that small pause to think instead of reacting defensively. The money I gave him, honestly, I won't miss, but it could have made an enormous difference to him.

So, here's my invitation to you: **The next time someone asks something of you, step into that thin space and allow yourself that second to think before you act. Live from your Magnificence.** Whether you say yes or no isn't as important as the fact that you thought about it instead of reacted from a place of self-protection.

The extent to which you do is the extent to which you'll be able to say, "I feel good about being me!"…and that's a promise!

A Bigger Picture

Years ago, I was diagnosed with a very rare blood disease (Eosinophilic Fasciitis, for those of you with curious minds). I honestly thought that I didn't have much longer to live. I wanted to make things easier for my wife and children, trying to get everything "in order." I was spending most of my days in bed, but could occasionally muster the energy to get up, dress, and go out into the world for a short time.

One of the things on my to-do list was getting the car inspected while I was still physically able. I saw this as being one less responsibility my wife would have if my disease progressed. We were living in a fairly rural area and I called the nearest inspection station to make an appointment. The woman who answered was very rude and treated me as if I was interrupting her morning. I thought she should be grateful that I was trying to give my business to her employer!

She told me that all the appointments were taken for the next couple of weeks, and she couldn't really give me a time when I might be able to come in for the inspection. I assured her that, as far as I knew, the car was in good shape; it just needed a new sticker.

She reiterated that she had no appointments available in the foreseeable future and told me I could call another time. I said some not nice things to her about how she represented a company in business to provide service, and adamantly told her that she wasn't doing her job well. In an ugly tone of voice, I told her that I wanted to speak to the owner! That's when she had the nerve to just hang up!

I felt angry, hurt, frustrated, insulted, and probably lots of other things as well.

I thought to myself, *if she knew I was dying, she wouldn't have treated me that way!*

Then I heard a voice from within speaking to me: *"If I knew SHE was dying, I wouldn't have treated her the way I did!"*

Wow!

Now my feelings were those of shame and embarrassment.

I tried to call back and apologize, but there was no answer...and the message box was full.

The short story is that my wife got the car inspected and I got well, but I never forgot the experience!

The truth is that I had no idea what was going on in her life at the time I called, and the more humbling truth is that I never gave it a thought. I sometimes forget that life isn't always just about ME!

We each have an Inner Magnificence, and we all deserve to be treated as such, even when we aren't feeling Magnificent and we, or they, don't act from that Magnificent place.

So, here's the invitation for today: **Treat everyone with the consideration you would have if you knew they were "terminally ill." Move into your Magnificence: Speak and react with that same kindness and compassion and understanding that you would want to receive.**

The extent you do is the extent to which you'll be able to say, "I feel good about being me!"...and that's a promise!

Football Rules

He was a good kid, an average student, and he got caught breaking the rules. He turned in a term paper and, as I read it, realized that he plagiarized a great deal of material. I don't like to fail students and I try to give everyone the benefit of the doubt. I returned his paper, saying that it was unacceptable because of the plagiarism. I tried to help him understand the rules about giving credit to the source of any material that he drew from beyond his own thinking. I gave him the opportunity to submit a second paper, trusting that he had learned his lesson.

When my student resubmitted his term paper, I was astonished to realize that he had clearly plagiarized significant portions of this paper as well. With sadness and curiosity, I confronted him and asked why he had done this? He responded by saying that he "thought he could get away with it." I explained to him that I didn't know what the ultimate consequences would be, but at the very least he would receive an "F" for the course.

In class we had gone over the work of Lawrence Kohlberg, who made significant contributions to the psychology of morality. Kohlberg suggested that there are several stages of moral development. The first stage is having a morality based on fear of being caught. In this stage, our thinking isn't so much about what is right, but what do we think we can get away with.

When I teach this material, I often use the example of football, and acknowledge that almost every football player, the linemen especially, are coached on how to hold and not get caught. The football players in the class smile smugly because their secret is out. Football has clear rules against holding an opponent, but the football morality is based, not so much on what is right, but on what a player can get away with.

I also use speeding as an example of the lowest level of morality. Most of us would drive faster than we do if we weren't afraid of getting caught; most of us admittedly drive over the speed limit, gauging our speed not so much on the actual speed limit, but rather how much over the speed limit we can drive before drawing the attention of the state police.

Kohlberg's second level of morality acknowledges that many people understand that for us to function in relationships of any kind there need to be rules. The third stage of morality recognizes that the rules of society work for most of the people, but sometimes there are extenuating circumstances that justify going outside the general rules. Moral decisions aren't always clearly black and white.

As you look at your life, what level of morality do you use for everyday living?

I would invite you to move into your Magnificence and **make decisions, not on what you think you can get away with, but on what is the right thing to do. Then do the right thing. Do the right thing every time!**

It is often much less convenient, but the extent to which you commit to always doing the right thing is the extent to which you'll be able to say, "I feel good about being me!"…and that's a promise!

His Name is Paul

W e have both worked at the same university for well over two decades. He is a full professor; I am an adjunct and we share the same office suite and mailroom. Over the years we've bumped into each other, smiled and nodded, and went our way.

The other day I was walking out of the office while he was walking in. He looked a bit distracted, so I said nothing and just kept on walking. That's when I heard a voice say, "Hi! How are you?" I turned around and he said, "I was distracted and failed to acknowledge you." I told him I was fine and asked how he was. You know; we followed the standard greeting protocol. Then we both smiled and went on about our day.

He's a big guy, close to a foot taller than I am. I know he is well-respected throughout the university community and, if I thought about it, I could easily allow myself to be intimidated.

A couple of days later, we ran into each other in the hallway and I did something very uncharacteristic. I looked at him and acknowledged, "I'm embarrassed to admit that I don't know your name." He smiled and said, "It's Paul. I'm Paul." I replied, "I'm Bary."

He stepped towards me a bit and said, "You know, you just did something I would never do!" He went on to concede that sometimes we work with people, we run into them often enough to make small talk. We share vacation stories, chat at the water cooler, but don't remember their names and are too embarrassed to admit it, because we've "known" them for so long.

He smiled and said, "I like your style!"

What I didn't tell him is that this really wasn't my style. I'm usually too worried about humiliating myself by saying something stupid. I don't like admitting that I don't know something that I think I should know. I don't know what possessed me to take a chance, but I'm glad I did! So was Paul!

I realize that when we allow ourselves to become more interested in connecting than we are in protecting our ego, life is better for everyone. When we stop worrying about what other people might think about us and we have the courage to make ourselves vulnerable, everybody wins.

I walked away, knowing we had made a connection. I left feeling good about myself for taking a chance. I like to think that maybe Paul might be emboldened to try it sometime himself.

Life really is about making connections. Our brains are hardwired to do that.

We have an Inner Magnificence that fills us with joy when we reach out and connect with people.

So, here's my invitation for today: **Be intentional about letting down your guard; be intentional about speaking to someone; allow yourself to be vulnerable enough to admit what you don't know, even when it feels awkward and a bit embarrassing.**

The extent to which you accept my invitation is the extent to which you'll be able to say, "I feel good about being me!"...and that's a promise!

Is Your Story Making You Sick?

As kids, we all liked to have somebody read us a story, especially if it was a way to put off bedtime. As soon as we learn to talk, we learn to make up stories. We tell stories of imaginary friends; we make up stories as feeble attempt to keep out of trouble. Sometimes our stories are about what we're going to be when we grow up, and sometimes our stores are our best attempt to understand what is happening to, and around, us.

It seems that we are hard-wired to tell stories. Stories are one of the most effective ways of communicating, getting, and holding people's attention. They help us connect on the intellectual and the emotional levels.

We each have our own series of stories. These are accounts we tell ourselves about ourselves. Sometimes we are the hero and sometimes we are the goat. Sometimes we are the victor and sometimes we are the victim!

What is important to know is that our lives are the products of the stories we tell ourselves about ourselves.

Have you noticed that people whose stories include "Things never go right for me." go through life with so much that doesn't go right? What they don't realize is that it is *their story* that is creating their life experiences.

Several years ago, I had a student who attended class regularly and was always engaged with the material we were covering. He and I were both surprised when he failed the first test. To his credit, he asked for an appointment to talk to me about it. When he first sat down, he announced, "I'm not a good student!" I asked him who told him that and right away he replied, "My second-grade teacher!" As we analyzed the questions he missed, I was struck by the fact that of the first five questions he missed, he originally had four of them correct, but he had gone back and changed his initial answers to incorrect ones.

I told him that he had spent the last ten-plus years believing a lie about himself. While I don't know that he would ever be an "A" student, I knew he was certainly a solid "B/C" student. I talked with him about how he was creating a reality based on his beliefs. I assured him that he was a good student, and I was going to believe in him until he believed in himself.

After the grades of the next test were posted, he came into class strutting like a peacock. He had made a B-, more than thirty points better than his first exam and all because he changed the story he told himself about being the kind of student he is. He now knows he is a "good" student."

What about you? What stories do you tell yourself? Stories of "can do" or stories of "can't do?" Henry Ford is credited as saying, "Whether you think you can or think you can't, you're probably right!" It is all because of your belief, your story.

I know that your story includes an Inner Magnificence that has potential far beyond what you have yet experienced.

My invitation for you today is **to edit carefully the stories you tell about your life. Move into your Magnificence and tell stories of possibility and potential, stories of success and power.**

The extent to which you do is the extent to which you'll be able to say, "I feel good about being me!"…and that's a promise!

Real People

When I was in seminary, I was the youth minister for a church a couple of hours away from campus. One of the couples in the congregation provided housing and meals for me each weekend. John was a machinist for the R.J. Reynolds Tobacco Company and Rachel was an inspector for the Hanes factory. They were the quintessential blue-collar couple.

On one occasion, the district superintendent and the bishop were coming to our church and Rachel offered to host the pastor, his family, and the guests for lunch after the Sunday service. I was surprised when I saw her on Saturday preparing the house for the dignitaries. She set up tables in the unfinished basement, got oilcloth table coverings, and put out paper plates, cups, and plastic utensils. I couldn't believe she wasn't using her china and silver, which I knew she had.

When I asked her about it, she said that these were interesting people and she was less concerned about impressing them than she was about having time for conversation with them. She told me that if she got out all the good stuff, she'd be spending time in the kitchen washing dishes and cleaning up when what she really wanted to do was have time to visit.

It made me question my values. I grew up being taught that when important people come to visit, you put out your best towels, you empty your wastebaskets, you get out your best dishes, and you get some fresh flowers to decorate. Oh yes, and you put on your best clothes.

Rachel realized that she wanted to enjoy her guests and she knew that doing all that decorating with fancy place settings wouldn't be fun. It would take away from her enjoyment, and it would ultimately deny her an opportunity to create much more than a superficial relationship based on how things looked.

How freeing! It never crossed her mind what her honored guests would think, and they were her honored guests! She was honoring them by wanting to connect with them by being real, instead of trying to impress them with appearances.

How about you? When you know you are going to have time with people who have social status, what's your goal? Do you want to impress them with how nice you can make things look, or do you want to get to know them on a personal level and develop a deeper relationship?

Rachel showed me that, for her, life is meant to be enjoyed to the fullest, not to impress people to the fullest. Sometimes it is fun to get out all the fancy china and silver, but other times we do it out of a sense of obligation instead of joy.

Here's my invitation for you: **The next time you have an opportunity to be around someone whose social status might be above yours, decide to enjoy their company instead of worrying about impressing them. Come from your Inner Magnificence and forget about your outer presentation.**

The extent to which you do is the extent to which you'll be able to say, "I feel good about being me!"...and that's a promise!

Taking Inventory

One Fourth of July weekend, we were driving through New Jersey on our way home from visiting family in West Virginia. As soon as we crossed into New Jersey, the informational highway signs read "All New Jersey Beaches Closed." As soon as I saw this, the cynical part of me said to my wife, "I bet that's Christie (New Jersey's governor) pulling some political stunt!"

It was only after arriving home and hearing the news that I got the story. If it wasn't bad enough to deny the citizens of New Jersey access to their own beaches, Gov. Christie was photographed with his family, enjoying one of those closed beaches. When confronted with the evidence, his response was something to the effect, "When you get elected governor, you can go to any beach you want!"

It seems to me that we have become a society where a sense of entitlement reigns. We have seen President Trump taking Air Force One on multiple golfing outings to Florida, seemingly oblivious to the taxpayers who are paying for his recreation. "I am the president, and I can do what I want to!" was his response to the criticism.

I saw it the other night as a National Grid crew was doing some roadwork. One guy was working the backhoe, one guy was shoveling like crazy, and three guys were sitting in the back of a truck watching. An hour and a half later, one guy was standing outside the truck (the "shoveler") and four guys were sitting in the back of the truck. A friend commented, "They're union. They can get away with that!"

Today I'm inviting each of us to look within ourselves. Alcoholics Anonymous calls it "taking a searching and fearless moral inventory of ourselves." When we look at the power that is ours, however great or small, do we use it for our personal advantage, or do we use it to make this a better world? What are we doing with our lives? Are we actively and purposefully making the world a better place, or are we selfishly making our own lives better in the moment? Are we living lives of service, or of privilege?

When we take that "searching and fearless moral inventory of ourselves," do we find any arrogance or sense of superiority? Are we operating from pride or humility?

I know that when I have a strong emotional reaction to something I see in the world around me, as I did when I saw the "Closed Beaches" sign, this reaction is my Inner Magnificence inviting me to look at myself and see in what ways I act similarly. How many times in my life have I done things just because I can, without thinking about the higher moral ground? I haven't thought about how my actions reflect on my position, nor have I thought about how my behavior might affect others. I've been focused only on what I wanted to do in the moment.

So, today I invite you to **join with me in taking that "fearless and searching moral inventory of ourselves." Instead of being purely self-serving, act in ways that reflect your Inner Magnificence and make the world a better place.**

The extent to which you accept my invitation is the extent to which you'll be able to say, "I feel good about being me!"…and that's a promise!

Values

I'm writing this from the deck of our timeshare overlooking the ocean in Falmouth, MA. I overheard a conversation among the folks on the other side of the privacy wall. They were talking about which ferry they would take out to Martha's Vineyard. Interestingly, before they could make that decision, they wanted to find out what time Mass was.

I was struck by the clarity of their value system. They were clear about "first things first." They were clear about not letting the world (the ferry schedule) control their lives. They were committed to making their lives revolve around their values (attending Mass).

I thought back to times when I did not have my life in proper order. It wasn't that I didn't have personal values, but rather that I allowed the pressure of the moment dictate my choices. I thought about times when an outside observer might not have been able to see what I contended my values were.

Many know the story of the Olympian Eric Liddell who, in the 1924 Olympics, had won every 100-meter race he ran, but when the gold medal race was scheduled to be run on a Sunday, he refused to run. For Liddell, Sunday was a day of rest, a Sabbath Day. Honoring his spiritual values was more important than his life-long dream of winning an Olympic gold medal.

When my children were in their teens, I would have told anyone who asked that they were my primary value, but I made decisions which made them feel like they were second, if even on my radar at all.

What I'm inviting us to think about is the extent to which we are so clear about what we value that we claim them first and make the world's schedule and demands fit around our values instead of the other way around. I know how easy it is to get caught in letting the demands of the world take control of how we live our lives, and then we look back and ask ourselves, "What happened?"

So, here's my invitation for today. It comes in four parts:

1) Take a few minutes and write down your three high-est/most important values. It doesn't matter what they are, just be unabashedly honest with yourself about what you truly value.

2) Look at the list and ask if you are proud of it; ask yourself if you would unashamedly show it to anyone. If so, proceed. If not, go back and make a list that you are proud to claim as your fundamental values.

3) Ask yourself whether an outsider observing your behavior would be able to discern your stated values, or would your behavior suggest something different?

4) Resolve to live your life around your values rather than living by the world's demands and timetable.

You have an Inner Magnificence. Let the world see it by the way you live your life. Let the world see evidence of it through every choice you make.

The extent to which you do is the extent to which you'll be able to say, "I feel good about being me!"...and that's a promise!

Well-Intended

I was at the supermarket the other day and I decided to do a good deed by taking a cart that someone had left in the lot, instead of simply getting one from inside the store. As I turned toward the store, I saw a woman sprawled on the ground in the driving lane. It took a moment for my brain to comprehend what I was seeing.

I'm a bit ashamed to admit that my first thought was to wonder if she was literally falling-down-drunk and then I realized it didn't matter. She was lying on the ground, was in danger of being run over, and needed help. I hurriedly pushed the cart towards her, fearing that if I just let it go, it might roll into someone's car.

As I got to her, asking if she was okay, ignoring the obvious that she was laying on the ground with a couple of grocery items beside her, a young man stopped his car, put it in park, jumped out and, grabbing the woman's arm, lifted her gently to her feet and asked if she needed help. She assured him that she was okay and that she had just turned her ankle somehow. He escorted the woman to her car, and I went on about my business.

As I thought about what just happened, I was disappointed in my reaction. I also thought about all the times when I have been aware

197

of someone in a difficult situation and, with the deepest sincerity, asked if there was anything I could do to help. Their response was typically, "Thanks, but I'm okay."

What struck me this time is that I stood there asking if there was something I could do while the other man, without asking, helped! I asked—he acted.

Sometimes what is needed is obvious, as in this case with the woman who had fallen and was on the ground. Sometimes the need isn't so obvious but, on some level, we know there is a need. Too often, I suspect, we don't look hard enough, or we are not thoughtful enough, to come up with a concrete action.

Very few of us are comfortable asking for help, even when it would make our lives better. Many of us pretend we're okay and muddle through, but it certainly makes life easier when someone jumps in and—without being asked—lends a helping hand.

We each have an Inner Magnificence that desires for us to feel good about ourselves. My research shows that we feel good about ourselves when we accomplish something and/or when we make a difference in the lives of others.

So, here's my invitation: **The next time you become aware of someone in need, someone dealing with a life challenge, don't just ask if there's something you can do. THINK of something you can do, and then do it!**

The extent to which you do is the extent to which you'll be able to say, "I feel good about being me!"…and that's a promise!

You Are Worthy

We flew across country to visit some friends and, when we arrived, they showed us to the bedroom where we always stay. They commented that the room probably hadn't been that neat since the last time we visited. They said, "It's good to have company occasionally; it's a good motivator!"

I couldn't help smiling, thinking of all the times when we know we are going to have company and we scurry around making everything look neat. All the wastebaskets get emptied, the counters are cleaned, the clutter put away; everything gets vacuumed and dusted. It all looks "nice" and "presentable," all ready to receive guests.

As I reflected on this, I had a couple of thoughts.

One was the irony that our friends were honoring us by making their house "presentable." In their eyes, we were worthy. On the other hand, if they were coming to visit us, we would do the same thing; we deem them worthy of making our home "presentable." We honor others by making our homes neat and orderly. The common thread is that we are all inherently worthy; we just don't always see ourselves in that light.

I know I'm a guy and I think like a guy, but I sometimes say to my wife that I'm not interested in living in something that looks like it came out of *Architectural Digest*. I'm comfortable having our home look and feel like we live here. I'm not invested in creating a "show place" for company.

On the other hand, if others see us as "honored guests," what keeps us from honoring ourselves by keeping our homes presentable? WE are worthy of living in that kind of space!

One possible reason why we would be embarrassed for others to see how we live is that we don't think WE are worthy of living in a space that is clean and orderly. WE don't honor ourselves the way we will honor our guests. If our living space isn't good enough for company, then it shouldn't be good enough for us either.

The other rationale for us being embarrassed for others to see how we really live is that we are more about presenting an image than we are about being real and being okay with who we really are.

I know there is middle ground between living in a constant mess and living in a model home, worthy of being featured in *Architectural Digest*, and I would invite us to think about where that is. Think about it: if the towels aren't good enough for guests, they probably aren't good enough for us either.

My wish for you is to remember that you have an Inner Magnificence and you already are worthy.

So, my invitation to you is two-fold: **1) Honor yourself the same way you would honor guests in your home, and 2) let your life be about being real instead of being concerned with an image.**

The extent to which you do is the extent to which you'll be able to say," I feel good about being me!"...and that's a promise!

Mediations and Meditations

Beyond a Sound Bite

Campaigning has already begun for the next mayoral election in our town and the very first poster I saw had the candidate promising to reduce taxes. That makes a great slogan and an enticing sound bite. No one is going to get elected with the promise that they will raise taxes.

My question, if I could ask the candidate, is "Where are you going to cut the budget?" Many of our roads are in desperate need of repair. Most of the school buildings are in serious need of modernization. We've had difficulty negotiating contracts with teachers, firefighters, and police officers. City pensions are underfunded. Which part of the operating budget are you going to cut?

I think that too often we victimize ourselves by listening to seductive sound bites. When a political candidate, or anyone, tells us something that we want to hear, it is easy to trust that they will deliver what they are promising, and never think twice about it.

We have an Inner Magnificence whose only purpose is to help us have everything in life that we call Good. It destines us for a life of joy, and it also requires something of us: it requires a thoughtful approach to

203

life…refusing ourselves the luxury of allowing someone else to do our thinking for us.

Life isn't about having someone tell us what we want to hear. Life is about listening for what is TRUE. When we look inward, seeking the TRUTH, we may not always like what we hear and see, but, as the scripture says, "You will know the truth and the truth will set you free!"

Freedom and joy are two sides of the same coin. When we are most free, we are also most joyous. The flip side is equally true: when we are most gullible, we are most likely to be hurt, to be disappointed, to be unhappy with the outcome.

I know, the truth isn't always pleasant at first, but it is constant and dependable. It is reliable and makes a solid foundation for a joyous life, and isn't that what we all want, a joyous life?

When we listen only to the sound bites, when we don't do our own thinking, when we cease thinking because we've heard words that resonate with a wounded part of us, or an angry part of us, that's when we lose our freedom and, ultimately, lose our joy.

Our Inner Magnificence has a truth meter, but we must look at it. We must be intentional about asking the deeper questions, the ones that connect us with the world as it really is as opposed to the world as we think we would like it to be. Sure, we'd all like to pay fewer taxes, but we need to ask ourselves about the consequences in the bigger picture of the services we want.

So, here's my invitation for you: **The next time you vote, do a "Reality Check" and vote for the candidate who has the courage to speak the TRUTH, not the candidate who offers the most seductive sound bites. Vote for the candidate who is acting from his or her Inner Magnificence instead of the one whose agenda is self-serving.**

The extent to which you do is the extent to which you'll move into your Magnificence and say, "I feel good about being me!"…and that's a promise!

Devolution?

I was at a Barnes and Noble bookstore recently and was struck by the number of books which include in their titles words which used to be considered profane. It caused me to wonder if we, as a society, as a culture are E-volving...or De-volving? Are we moving into our highest and best, or are we sliding into a lower version of what is meant to be human?

I am uncertain sometimes in the difference between making an observation and making a judgment. No doubt, many of you will read this as a judgment and, if it is, this is simply a reflection of my values, and I'm okay with that.

Books with titles containing the phrases "Kick Ass" or "Bad Ass" have become popular bestsellers; I know, because I have a couple of them in my library. I am privileged to know, and have great respect for, the authors! There are books whose titles contain the word "Sh*t" or "F*ck," as in *How to Stop Feeling Like Sh*t*, and *Get Your Sh*t Together*. Then there is the bestseller, *The Subtle Art of Not Giving a F*ck*, and *Go the F*ck to Sleep!* Oh, and don't forget "Bitch" and "Skinny Bitch." There are lots more—trust me, I've done my research! I've also been told that this book should have an edgier title; that *Move into Your Magnificence* is too soft. Oh, well!

One of the other things I've noticed is that most of the books with titles like this are in the "Self-Help" section of the bookstore!

So, what's up with that?

I get it—at least I think I do. It's about marketing. It's about attention getting. It's about shock value. It is a strategy which has certainly served to make people like Howard Stern millions of dollars as a "shock jock!" It can be argued that the use of shocking language has become a successful marketing strategy, spring-boarding books into Best-Seller status.

For me this raises the question, since we are in the Self-Help genre, are we really helping ourselves by normalizing language like this? Does language like this help us connect to our Inner Magnificence, or does it serve to anchor us solidly in the mentality of our current culture? Does it help us to move to a higher plane of consciousness, or sink us to a baser level?

Maybe I'm old-fashioned—wait; there is no "maybe" here. I AM old-fashioned and that skews my perspective. I believe the current state of affairs in our nation, and in our world, calls for a level of civility, a level of politeness, a level of discourse which unites rather than shocks.

Language like this might make us more money, but does it make us better people? Does it help us e-volve, or are we participating in the cultural process of de-volving?

I believe it is a question worthy of conversation, and that's all I'm asking for.

So, my invitation is for you to **look at your Inner Magnificence and ask yourself whether the way you are presenting yourself—or your product—reflects your true Magnificence, or is it more of a reflection of the current cultural values?**

The extent to which you do is the extent to which you'll be able to say, "I feel good about being me!"…and that's a promise!

For or Against?

R ecently I had a conversation with a former colleague about how the younger generation is different from our generation. I suspect that every generation has that conversation; I certainly know my parents' generation did.

As we were talking, I realized a consistent pattern: When we go through our adolescent rebellion, we become clear about what we are against! We protest, just like many of my generation protested the Vietnam War, and in our protesting, in our against-ness, we treated the Vietnam veterans badly, shamefully! Currently, we are living in a political climate of protesting perceived societal wrongs, and certainly there are many!

My contention is that as our thinking matures, we begin to talk about what we are for, instead of what we are against. It isn't enough to know what we don't want; we need to know what we do want. Eliminating one option is helpful, to an extent, but the real power comes in claiming what we are for, rather than what we are against.

In my adolescence, I was against the idea of God. I reasoned that if God existed, and if God is loving, how could God allow so much suffering? It didn't make sense to me. I was against the church. I saw so

207

much hypocrisy. I saw so many people who professed one thing on Sunday and who lived by a separate set of values during the week. I was against some of the cornerstone teachings of the church; the notion of a "Virgin Birth," for example, contradicted everything I knew about science, as did other literal interpretations of scripture.

Recognizing what we are against may be the first step in our development. Think of the favorite word of a two-year-old: NO! However, we have an Inner Magnificence that isn't against anything, but it is always FOR things. My generation was for Peace, but few of us stopped to think about what peace would look like, perhaps because, to a substantial extent, we were an angry generation. Then, as our thinking continued to mature, we realized that peace isn't just the absence of war; peace is a state of mind.

This realization connects us to something powerful and something we can control: the creation of a peaceful state of mind. That is a condition we can all be for! That is a position which both reflects and reveals our Inner Magnificence. That is a force that is earth-changing!

Maybe the starting point for us needs to be naming what we are against, but our influence becomes greatly enhanced when we can articulate what we are for, and even more significant when we learn to become that for which we stand and proclaim.

So, here's my invitation for today: **Instead of cataloguing what you are against and profusely posting your position online; decide to move into your Magnificence; proclaim what you are for and, finally, decide to become peaceful, joyous, loving, harmonious, and all the qualities which you label as good... Godly, even!**

The extent to which you do is the extent to which you'll be able to say, "I feel good about being me!"...and that's a promise!

Help!

Maybe it's my age, or my eyes, or both, but sometimes when I'm working on a document on my computer, I have trouble finding the cursor. I've been frustrated with this for some time now. But today when I was on campus in the library at a writers' retreat, it occurred to me that the "Help Desk" for computers is on the main level.

I went down and told the student covering the department what my problem was and, with a few clicks on the keyboard, he not only fixed it for me, he showed me how I could change it for myself, making the cursor bigger or smaller, even changing its color! He told me it's easy.

I jokingly remarked, "Everything is easy, if you know how!" He smiled.

This is true of life: No matter what it is, it is easy if you know how. This applies to everything from sharpening a pencil to flying a 747. That may be a bit simplistic, because there are some things that, even when you know how, can be extremely challenging.

For me, pride gets in the way. I tell myself that I should be able to figure things out. After all, I'm a smart guy. It is like the classic joke about men unwilling to ask for directions: It's not a "manly" thing to do.

We have to put aside our pride to admit that we are lost, that we don't know how to do something, that we need help.

Yet, how much easier life is when we *are* willing to ask for help, when we are willing to admit that we don't know everything. There is very little about which we know everything.

That's part of what makes life fun: learning new things, solving problems, figuring things out. But I'm here to say that sometimes asking for help makes life so much easier and fun! That's part of what makes the university community so attractive to me; it is full of people who take great delight in learning and in helping

In the computer lab, there was a student sitting all alone at the help desk, just waiting for someone to come with a problem to be solved. Here at this retreat are folks from the writing center and reference librarians, not to mention colleagues who all seem to enjoy helping by sharing their expertise and their perspective.

We know how flattering it is when someone comes to us and asks for our expertise, when someone acknowledges that we know something that they don't, and they seek our help.

What I know is that, for me, it is so much easier to give help than it is to ask for it.

I guess that's the choice: Do we want to make our lives easier by asking for, and accepting, help, or stubbornly struggle because we have too much pride to admit that there is something we don't know.

So, here's my invitation: Move into Your Magnificence. **Put aside your pride and take advantage of all the resources around you. Just as you enjoy helping others, allow others to enjoy helping you.**

The extent to which you accept my invitation is the extent to which you'll be able to say, "I feel good about being me!"…and that's a promise!

Next!

S ometimes when I meet couples, I ask them how they met, or how they got together. I end up hearing wonderful stories. When I did that the other day, the couple—somewhat sheepishly—admitted that it was through an online dating service. They shared with me their experiences with the dating site.

She commented that she learned a lot about herself when she put herself out there in the world of online dating. When I asked what she learned, she said that she had to come to terms with the feeling of rejection. She talked about how long it took her to realize that she wasn't being rejected— because the men on the dating site swiping left didn't know the real her at all! What they were rejecting was the conclusions they drew about her, based on a photograph.

She is a bright woman, successful in her profession and independent. She doesn't use a lot of makeup; she wears glasses and has her hair pulled back in a ponytail.

We joked about what the men were rejecting wasn't her at all. They were saying no to her marketing presentation. They were rejecting the image and the conclusions they drew from her profile picture. She wasn't putting herself out there as a sexy blonde; she was just being herself. The reality is that they knew only a tiny fraction of one percent of the person she is. What they knew was what her profile picture looked like.

That got me to thinking about the whole concept of rejection, because a lot of what we don't try in life comes from a fear of rejection. Jack Canfield maintains that there is no such thing as rejection, and here is his logic: If you ask for something and don't get it, you didn't have it before, so you are no worse off. When we ask somebody for something, whether it is asking for a favor or asking them to buy something, they are either going to say "Yes," "No," or "Let me think about it."

The point I want to make is that rejection is not one of the options. Even if someone responds with a "swipe left" which means "no" on dating sites like Tinder and Bumble (I know this because I watched a TEDx Talk by a Bryant alumnus), they haven't rejected the other person; they simply said, "No."

Rejection is a concept that exists in our heads, and when someone says no to a request of ours, we take it personally and feel rejected.

When any successful sales person hears a no, they simply say "Next," and move on. It isn't about feeling rejected; it is about looking for a yes.

We each have an Inner Magnificence and—here's the truth—no one who ever truly sees our Magnificence would ever reject it! Our Inner Magnificence always exudes universally attractive qualities.

So, here's my invitation: **Don't let the fear of rejection keep you from asking for what you want—even if it is through an online dating service—and if someone responds with a no to your request, respond from your Magnificence and simply say, "Next!"**

When you realize that YOU can't be rejected, you will be able to say, "I feel good about being me!"…and that's a promise!

The Power of One

"*I* *am only one, but I am one. I cannot do everything, but I can do something. And because I cannot do everything, I will not refuse to do the something that I can do.*" According to Wikipedia, those are the words of Edward Everett Hale, an American author, historian, and Unitarian clergyman. He was a child prodigy who exhibited extraordinary literary skills. At the age of thirteen, he was enrolled at Harvard University where he graduated second in his class.

We are at a time in this country when most of our citizens are fundamentally opposed to some of the policies and practices of our government, particularly at the federal level. Rather than responding to the combined voices of the masses, the president and his cabinet, along with the majority of Congress, seem to be pursuing an agenda of lining the pockets of the wealthy at the expense of the lower and middle-class. Some of the legislation and current implementation of policies appears abhorrent to the majority.

The average citizen seems frustrated and increasingly angry as this administration continues to pursue a self-centered agenda, an agenda that is not for the benefit of the average citizen, but for the privileged few.

This past weekend, the president's Press Secretary was denied service by the owner of a D.C. restaurant. Meanwhile, the head of the

Department of Homeland Security was hounded out of a Mexican restaurant in Washington because of the way her department is choosing to enforce immigration policy. They weren't denied because of race or sexual orientation; they weren't denied because of ethnic background, age, or gender. They were denied because of their behavior.

We each have an Inner Magnificence that, when we attend to it, energizes us to draw attention to matters of truth and justice, to matters of compassion and understanding. We have an Inner Magnificence that reflects all that is noble and lofty, good and pure.

Rather than allowing themselves to feel victimized by a sense of powerlessness in the face of falsehoods and deception and cruelty, we have examples of individuals who are adopting Hale's proclamation that, even though they are only one, and even though they can't do everything, they are claiming the "something" they can do and doing it.

What about you? When you become aware of something that offends your sense of goodness, what do you do? Do you assume the victim posture, and justify it by telling yourself that you are only one person and there isn't anything you can do? Or, do you look within and claim the power you have, however much or little it may seem? Do you let the fact that you can't do everything stop you from doing the something that you can do? When we make that choice, we end up robbing ourselves, because we have chosen not to honor our own Magnificence.

So, here's my invitation for today: **Honor your Inner Magnificence. When you become aware of a situation that doesn't reflect the best of humanity, choose to *do something*. Refuse to excuse your inaction by telling yourself that you are only one person. Claim your power and act on it!**

The extent to which you do is the extent to which you will say, "I feel good about being me!"…and that's a promise!

TV Fast

Off and on during my life journey, I've experimented with fasting. I felt better when I did it, but fasting demands a certain kind of focus. Over a recent weekend I went on a different kind of fast: a TV fast. That's right; I never turned on the TV for over twenty-four hours.

It wasn't intentional in the beginning, but it was by the end of the day. My wife and I were visiting another part of the country. We were in and out, enjoying a day of fun and exploring the area. It was later in the day that my habit of turning on the TV surfaced.

I made a conscious choice not to give in to the habit. It wasn't easy! I'm a sports fan and somewhat of a news junkie.

Looking at the blank screen on the TV meant that I didn't check the news, or the weather. It meant that I missed some of the Stanley Cup playoffs, the Red Sox, AND the Kentucky Derby, not to mention my standard reality shows of "Alaskan State Troopers" or "Alaska: The Last Frontier" or "North Woods Law." (My fascination with Alaska and law enforcement is fodder for another time.)

I was resisting the urge to turn on the TV and channel surf until I found something that caught my attention when I had one of those "Aha!" moments: I realized that I wasn't missing anything of significance for my life. Sports events happen whether I'm there or not. They play whether I'm emotionally invested or not. Reality shows are scripted; they aren't as spontaneous as they portray themselves to be. And as for news, anything that affects me directly won't need the TV to make itself known.

So, I spent the evening reading a novel and enjoyed being with my wife as she worked on a Sudoku puzzle. It was very relaxing, inspiring, and thought-provoking. How's that for a good way to spend an evening!

The question for me becomes, "What would I do with myself if I didn't have TV?" My hunch is that I would be more creative. I would probably read more and maybe do more writing. I would be more productive. My brain would be more active and engaged, instead of being passively distracted.

I am sure that my life overall would be richer and more meaningful if I were to choose more evenings like that and fewer evenings numbing myself in front of the TV.

We have an Inner Magnificence that invites us to feel alive, that doesn't want to be hidden behind the mesmerizing screen of some TV.

So here's my invitation: **Try it for yourself, no TV for twenty-four hours.** Share your experience with me. If you're like me, it won't be easy. You might find yourself at loose ends, but that's the point. The TV void will give you time to find yourself and to connect with what is inside rather than what the TV imposes.

The extent to which you accept my invitation is the extent to which you'll be able to say, "I feel good about being me!"...and that's a promise!

Now, to deal with my attachment to my cell phone!

Wants vs. Needs

I grew up in a gun culture. I bought my own BB gun when I was nine. We lived out in the country and I spent lots of time shooting it. One of my most memorable birthdays was my twelfth! My dad took me to the local pawn shop and bought me a 20-gauge shotgun! Some of my best memories of adolescence were going hunting with my dad.

As an adult, I bought a 30-06 Winchester hunting rifle and made my own ammunition. Shooting is fun! I get it! Pulling the trigger on a machine gun is quite a kick! (Pun intended!) I don't want to deprive anyone of that experience.

However, I have yet to have anyone give me a rational explanation as to why they **need to own** a weapon that can shoot forty to sixty rounds a minute, or more! Maybe the military— that's a different story— but I'm talking about regular law-abiding citizens.

I do know friends and family members who WANT to own weapons like this, but here's the rub: When the "wants" of a small number of people come in conflict with the needs of the larger society, then it seems to me that we need to deny our wants for the greater good.

CBS reported that six weeks into 2018, there were already eighteen school shootings in this country. We are the ONLY COUNTRY in the world dealing with this epidemic of carnage to our children.

It seems that we would be well-served to look at what other countries are doing, and learn something. They've figured out something that we haven't. They have figured out how to keep their children safe when they go to school!

It is easy to point the finger and place blame. It is easy to offer platitudes like "Guns don't kill; people kill." I guarantee that if dozens of our school children had died this year from an infectious disease, we would be pouring massive amounts of money into research, but when it is a white guy with a semi-automatic rifle, we shake our heads and wonder what part of the system failed, and we offer to pray for the families.

I want my grandchildren to feel safe when they go to school. I don't want them leaving home in the morning, wondering if what has happened to so many other schools might happen in theirs. I don't want anybody's children to be afraid to go to school for fear of being shot! Some of the things that have changed drastically in my lifetime are the huge increase in the availability and number of guns, and their destructive power.

Why is it that we seem unwilling to even look at what other countries are doing differently? My hunch is that deep down, we have a fear that when we do look, we will realize that many of us will need to give up some of what we want for the greater good of what our children and what our society need. More people with more guns have not made our country safer; they have made our schools, our malls, our movie theaters and public places deadlier.

My invitation is for each of us to live from our Inner Magnificence and honor the Magnificence of our children. My invitation is for us to start thinking, not what do I want, but what do our children need? My invitation is to stop pointing fingers at who and what

is to blame and to start thinking, "What can I do to make this world a better place for our children?"

The extent we do is the extent to which we will be able to say, "I feel good about being me!"…and that's a promise!

What's on Your "Not to Do" List?

I confess I have somewhat of an addiction to Facebook. My wife would ask me to drop the qualifier and just admit outright that I am an addict! Time after time, she will see me scrolling through and ask, "What are you learning?"

I must admit that I'm not learning *anything*. I don't go to Facebook to *learn;* I go to Facebook to be entertained. Facebook is a sort of voyeuristic entertainment that allows me to see what other people are doing, or pictures of their "cute" pets, or amusing clips of people doing stupid things. There are times, however, when I do come across informative pieces. Sometimes these are inspirational quotes. Other times "teaser" ads pop up for an educational "How To" program that someone is selling, and they offer a free webinar as an enticement.

I was talking with a friend the other day who shared that Facebook was the same "hook" for her attention. She, like me, would vow to limit her time scrolling, only to find herself becoming engrossed in whatever post was coming up next.

She has developed a mantra to address this condition. She asks herself, "Is what I'm doing helping me achieve the goals I set for today?" Of course, the answer is almost always, "No!" The problem, she confessed, is that too often she has already lost a significant amount of time before the mantra kicks in.

What she and I share is the awareness that some of our habits don't serve us. We know that they are "time thieves." They suck up time and leave us with virtually nothing to show. They have not moved us forward in our life plan and goals one iota.

To be successful, to have a sense of accomplishment with our day, with our lives, sometimes what we choose NOT to do can be even more powerful than choosing what TO do.

I think AA has it right: One day at a time. Each morning when we get up, we make a commitment that—at least for today—I am not going to _____. In the case of AA, we fill in the blank with "drink," but we each have our own habits and behaviors that do not serve us in the larger picture. It isn't even that these habits are harmful; they just don't serve us.

What about you? Do you have any habits like this? Do you have habits that serve to mindlessly pass time?

AA teaches us that we shouldn't "take anyone else's inventory," which means that it isn't up to us to decide what other people ought to be doing—or not doing. It is up to us to take an honest look at our daily life, to be aware of the behaviors that serve us, that move us towards the life we'd like to have and those which simply serve as distractions.

So, here's my invitation for today: **Tap into your Inner Magnificence. Take an honest look at how you spend your day and make a conscious decision about what you are NOT going to do today, so that you will have time to do what will enrich your life.**

The extent to which you do is the extent to which you'll be able to say, "I feel good about being me"…and that's a promise!

Will the Real Story Get Hijacked?

Some time ago, United Airlines received much unwanted publicity for the very forcible tactics used in removing Dr. David Dao from an overbooked flight from Chicago to Louisville, KY. They needed the space to get four United crew members to their assignments.

The incident stirred up much conversation around the whole issue of "passengers' rights" when an airline overbooks a flight. It has also caused a publicity nightmare for the airline in the way they chose to handle the situation. The legalities are being sorted out and clarified and consciousness is being raised around the almost-never-read contract we implicitly sign when we purchase an airline ticket.

In my opinion, that should have been the story: the fine print of the contract we never see, let alone read, and the way big business is sometimes more self-serving and how they sometimes abuse consumers.

What is troublesome to me is that the reporter covering the story decided to investigate Dr. Dao's personal history, and that made the headlines. More than ten years ago, he was found guilty of medical malpractice and had his license revoked. In the years since, he has fastidiously worked to regain the trust of the licensing board and has been reinstated.

What does ANY of that have to do with what happened on that airplane?

Who among us hasn't done things that have caused us embarrassment? For some of us, those behaviors have been made very public. Others simply carry the shame and guilt inwardly.

The real question for us is: What do we do with information we have about someone's past?

Will that forever define how we think about them, or will we give them the benefit of the doubt and acknowledge that they have learned some painful life lesson(s)? Will the story we tell be about what someone did or didn't do in the past, or will it celebrate who they are today?

Will we allow that person to live from their potential, or will we be a part of making sure the world knows? How we deal with what we know or discover about someone else's past reflects on our character.

Recently, I learned that decades ago a friend fathered a son out of wedlock. Now, he is happily married with a couple of children. Do I allow myself to see him for the man, husband, and father he is now, or is my perspective colored by something that happened years ago? Another friend served time in prison for DUI, death resulting. I have yet another friend who would make a wonderful government leader, but he won't allow himself to even be nominated because he made some regrettable decisions in the past, and he knows the news will dig it up and put it out for public consumption. The real story isn't about what happened then, it is about how he lives now.

The question for reflection is what we choose to do when we learn about a chapter in someone's past that they would like to put behind them.

Knowing that we each have an Inner Magnificence, and knowing that we don't always act from that place, can we choose to live in the present and let others do the same?

The real story shouldn't have been about Dr. Dao's past, but how he was treated by United Airlines.

So, here's my invitation: **Move into your Magnificence and truly live in the present and allow others to do the same. Refuse to contaminate this day by sharing information about someone else that doesn't come from a place of love and support.**

223

The extent to which you accept my invitation is the extent to which you'll be able to say, "I feel good about being me!"...and that's a promise!

Retirement

I'm writing this as the spring semester is ending and summer break is on the horizon. My wife used to ask me when I am going to retire. My stock answer is, "Either, when I'm not having fun, or when the student evaluations tell me I'm no longer effective."

I am fortunate to have a job that I love, except for when I'm facing a stack of term papers that can be several inches high. (I enjoy reading the good ones, but the others are tedious and seldom interesting; sometimes there seems to be more of "the others.")

My dad took early retirement, and, I believe, that was the beginning of a slow, down-hill slide into the darkness of dementia. Several years into his retirement, and dementia, he had a moment that was crystal clear. He looked at me and said, "Bary, you have to have something to retire to, not just something to retire from." That was perhaps the wisest advice he ever gave me.

Do you know that some languages don't even have a word for retirement? The concept is so foreign that there is no word in their vocabulary.

Sarah Laskow wrote in the Oct. 24th, 2014 edition of *The Atlantic* that "when the Social Security Act was passed in 1935, the official retirement age was 65. Life expectancy for American men was around 58 at the time." At that time, the idea of retirement really had to do with life expectancy, and for those who lived well past the average lifespan, the assumption was that they would be ill or otherwise disabled and would need supplemental financial resources.

We have an Inner Magnificence that thrives on activity, on a sense of contribution to others, and of doing something meaningful.

I get that not everybody enjoys their job, the task that "pays the bills." I get that some people feel trapped and can't wait to retire! What I'm suggesting is that we change our focus from what it is that we want to quit doing and focus on what it is that we could do that would give our lives meaning and a sense of accomplishment.

You don't even have to wait until you get to retirement age to do it. You can begin now.

So, here's my invitation: **If you love your work, do it as long as you enjoy it and are competent at it. If you don't love your work, then begin thinking about what you would love to be doing that will give you a sense of purpose, of accomplishment, of making a difference. What gives you joy and makes you feel alive? It may, or may not, pay the bills, but it will enrich your life.**

The extent to which you fill your life with meaningful work is the extent to which you'll be able to say, "I feel good about being me!"…and that's a promise!

Saving Our Planet – the Arrogance of It All

By NASA's calculations, the earth is a little over four and a half
billion years old. Read that again: four and a half BILLION years!
We homo sapiens have been on the scene for about two hundred
thousand years, which turns out to be 0.0000444 of the time. In addition,
we humans have only been industrialized about two hundred and fifty
years, or 0.00125 of that ... and we are arrogant enough to think that we
have some control over the earth's survival!

Very few of us, it seems, have realized that we humans are one
organism which lives on this planet. As far as the planet is concerned, we
are just like viruses and bacteria, just like the various plants and animals.
What we've forgotten is that everything we do affects everyone and
everything else in the world, in big or small ways.

The planet isn't going to die because we in the United States
throw away plastic bottles at the rate of one thousand five hundred every
second. The fact is that seventy percent of these that go into landfills and
will slowly degrade; that process will take about a thousand years.
Recycling doesn't even scratch the surface; we need learn to use
significantly less plastic, but whatever we decide to do, or not do, the
planet will survive.

227

It is we – the human species – which is endangered.

So, what is the remedy? It is going to require us to lose our "independent man" mentality. It is going to require us to truly grasp that we are one. It is going to require us to stop thinking about what we want as individuals; we need to stop thinking only about what is good for me and start thinking about what is good for the whole of us.

The only way we, as a species, are going to survive is for us to realize that what really matters is what we have in common, not what makes us different. The differences make us interesting, but at this moment in history what matters is our commonality.

Years ago, in Sunday School I learned a song: "Red and Yellow, Black and White, we are precious in His sight…" Whether we do it through our spirituality, our philosophy, or our science, unless and until we realize that we are all interconnected, we are all doomed … but the planet will go on!

My invitation for today is much more challenging than reducing your use of plastic or figuring out what to put in the recycling bin. It is to move into Your Magnificence and make the conscious decision to see the Inner Magnificence within EVERY face you see. Be courageous enough to ask how you can be respectful … in EVERY action, EVERY decision, and EVERY word that comes out of your mouth. This is how you can affect the world. The human race will be saved to the extent to which we learn to live in harmony with each other and our environment. As for the planet … it's just fine!

The extent to which you accept my invitation is the extent to which you'll be doing your part to save the human species. It is the extent to which you'll be able to say, "I feel good about being me!" … and that's a promise.

If you are looking for an inspirational speaker, a workshop leader, or a personal success coach, please feel free to contact me at:

Bary@DrBaryFleet.com
www.DrBaryFleet.com

If you like what you've read in this book, I have some FREE GIFTS FOR YOU.

Go to www.DrBaryFleet.com/BookBonuses.
Enter your email address and I will send you:

1) A Downloadable audible copy of this book.
2) A set of five more recent articles including:
   a. *Who are You Becoming*
   b. *A Trail of Litter: What Does Yours Look Like?*
   c. *The Price of Convenience*
   d. *A Million Little Things*
   e. *The Shame I Carry*
3) Check my Coaching Page and register for a FREE thirty-minute coaching session.

Remember: If I can ever be of service to you, please don't hesitate to reach out!

There's nothing I'd like to do more than to help you or your organization

connect with
YOUR INNER MAGNIFICENCE!

CPSIA information can be obtained
at www.ICGtesting.com
Printed in the USA
LVHW011759230420
654342LV00005B/1192